Theorizing Ocean Governance: a Framework Combining Governance, Science, and Law

The Law of the Sea

Volumes published in this Brill Research Perspectives title are listed at *brill.com/rplss*

Theorizing Ocean Governance: a Framework Combining Governance, Science, and Law

By

Lena Schøning

BRILL

LEIDEN | BOSTON

Library of Congress Control Number: 2024946723

Typeface for the Latin, Greek, and Cyrillic scripts: "Brill". See and download: brill.com/brill-typeface.

ISSN 2667-3398
ISBN 978-90-04-72025-1 (paperback)
ISBN 978-90-04-72026-8 (e-book)
DOI 10.1163/9789004720268

Contents

Theorizing Ocean Governance: a Framework Combining Governance, Science, and Law

Lena Schøning

Abstract

Ocean governance is emerging as a field of study on its own, traversing the three knowledge domains of governance, science, and law. The vast literature on ocean governance is however scattered across multiple publication channels, which challenges theory building in this field. This study aims to instigate further discussion on the theory of ocean governance, by conceptualizing a governance perspective that systematizes governance into three components: structures and processes; ideals and standards; and substance or merits. The relevance of science and law to each of these components is investigated, resulting in a nuanced discussion on the diverse yet limited ways that science influences governance (the science–policy interface) and the many and vital roles of law for governance.

Keywords

ocean governance – science–policy interface – governance–law interface – science-based decision-making – science of actionable knowledge

1 Introduction

1.1 *Background*

The relationships of governance, science, and law are high on the ocean governance agenda. The United Nations (UN) Decade of Ocean Science for Sustainable Development (2021–2030) aims to "bridge science, policy, and societal dialogue"[1] and states that "[a]daptation strategies and science-informed policy responses to global change are urgently needed."[2] The 2022 Kunming-Montreal

1 UNESCO-IOC, *The Science We Need for the Ocean We Want*, Intergovernmental Oceanographic Commission (Paris, France, 2020).

2 United Nations Decade of Ocean Science for Sustainable Development (2021–2030), source: https://en.unesco.org/ocean-decade (last accessed 25 April 2023).

 | DOI:10.1163/9789004720268_002

Global Biodiversity Framework sets out that "[I]mplementation of the framework requires transformative, innovative and transdisciplinary education, formal and informal, at all levels, including science–policy interface studies."[3] A central legal framework relevant to ocean governance, and often referred to as the constitution of the ocean,[4] is the UN Convention on the Law of the Sea (UNCLOS)[5] and multiple states have recently concluded in legal terms how to govern the high seas.[6] Both of these legal frameworks refer to the use of the science.[7]

Yet, the actual relationships between governance, science, and law are not straightforward, especially in the context of ocean governance, with a deteriorating marine environment, an increasing demand for ocean spaces and resources for food, energy, and transportation, embedded in intricate governance and legal structures. As per MacDonald et al., "[g]iven the current and future threats facing the oceans (…) we cannot act soon enough to remedy the challenges at the science–policy interface(s)."[8] Cosens et al. conclude that the "response to modern rapid drivers of change (such as climate change) requires research (…) and understanding of governance, law, and science as integrated knowledge systems."[9] McConney et al. state how "[a]ddressing the science–policy interface is key to governance reform" and necessitates "investigations from around the world [that] highlight the urgent need to repair or strengthen marine science–policy interfaces in ocean governance."[10]

---

3 UN/CBD/COP/15/L25, "Kunming-Montreal Global Biodiversity Framework," 2022.

4 For example, as per Natalie Klein and Kate Parlett, *Judging the Law of the Sea* (Oxford, UK: Oxford University Press, Incorporated, 2023): 4, "UNCLOS has long been described as the 'constitution of the oceans'."

5 United Nations Convention on the Law of the Sea (UNCLOS), adopted 10 December 1982, entered into force 16 November 1994, 1833 UNTS 397.

6 Agreement under the United Nations Convention on the Law of the Sea on the conservation and sustainable use of marine biological diversity of areas beyond national jurisdiction, adopted 19 June 2023, not yet entered into force (High Seas Biodiversity Treaty). This agreement is referred to by some as the BBNJ Agreement.

7 UNCLOS art 119; High Seas Biodiversity Treaty art 7 (i).

8 Bertrum H. MacDonald et al., *Science, information, and policy interface for effective coastal and ocean management* (Boca Raton, Fla.: CRC Press, 2016), 463.

9 Barbara Cosens et al., "Governing complexity: Integrating science, governance, and law to manage accelerating in the commons," *Proceedings of the National Academy of Sciences—PNAS* 118, no. 36 (2021): 3, 2102798118. These authors hold that system theory is crucial for a deeper understanding, while this study argues for the necessity of multiple different perspective.

10 Patrick McConney et al., "A First Look at the Science-Policy Interface for Ocean Governance in the Wider Caribbean Region," *Frontiers in Marine Science* 2 (2016): 14, fmars.2015.00119.

To the extent that theoretical advancement of the governance–science and governance–law relationships may further ocean governance practice, understanding and clarifying these relationships becomes important.

This study approaches ocean governance both as an area of practiced governance and as a set of thematic and theoretical perspectives reflecting a field of study. As an area of practiced governance, 'ocean governance' is evident, for example, in national and international policy initiatives, such as in national marine governance plans and policies,[11] the high-level multinational panel for a sustainable ocean economy,[12] and the UN Ocean Conferences.[13] Naming these and similar practices as 'ocean governance' may reflect a recent trend. Yet, some of these practices, such as the management of maritime activities and marine resources, are as old as nation states and beyond. Other ocean governance practices may rather reflect emerging ways of interaction, such as some national cross-sectoral policies (e.g., marine spatial plans), some international networks and panels (e.g., the High Level Panel for a Sustainable Ocean Economy), and some conferences (e.g., Our Ocean conferences).

As a set of thematic and theoretical perspectives, ocean governance is emerging as a field of study in its own right. It includes multidisciplinary topics concerning intertwined knowledge domains and themes, such as governance, science, and law, across the boundaries of traditional disciplines.[14] For example, scholarship on ocean governance frequently refers to components of governance (such as coordination,[15] adaptivity,[16] and management

---

11 For example, as per the International Marine Spatial Planning (MSP) forum and the MSP global Initiative, about 100 countries/territories now have MSP initiatives, source: https://www.mspglobal2030.org/about/ (last accessed 25 April 2023).

12 Source: https://oceanpanel.org (last accessed 25 April 2023).

13 Source: https://www.un.org/en/conferences/ocean2022 (last accessed 25 April 2023).

14 As per Charles Ehler, Jacek Zaucha, and Kira Gee, "Maritime/Marine Spatial Planning at the Interface of Research and Practice," 614, in *Maritime Spatial Planning: Past, present, future*, ed. Jacek Zaucha and Kira Gee (Cham: Palgrave Macmillan, 2019): 2, "The imperative for employing a multidisciplinary approach stems from the nature of marine space as a multi-dimensional concept requiring insight from many scientific disciplines and types of knowledge."

15 Anthony Charles, "People, oceans and scale: governance, livelihoods and climate change adaptation in marine social–ecological systems," *Current Opinion in Environmental Sustainability* 4, no. 3 (2012): 351–57, 352; Karen N. Scott, "Integrated Oceans Management: A New Frontier in Marine Environmental Protection," in *Oxford Handbook of the Law of the Sea*, ed. Donald R. Rothwell et al. (Oxford: Oxford University Press, 2015): 463, 467.

16 The "adaptability inherent in zoning may be the single most important weapon in our armoury to achieve effective, efficient and equitable management of resources," alongside strategic planning, as per Tundi S. Agardy, *Ocean Zoning: Making Marine Management More Effective* (London, UK: Taylor & Francis Group, 2010): 6. Reiterated by Catarina

processes[17]), to science as the basis for governance (such as in science-based approaches or science-based decision-making),[18] and to the necessity of law (such as in the need for implementation in legal instruments or for not jeopardizing the rule of law).[19]

Scholarly literature extensively covers the thematic and theoretical perspectives on ocean governance, yet is scattered across multiple and diverse publication channels, which challenges theory building in this field. Therefore, this study aims to instigate further discussion on, and development of, the theory of ocean governance. The literature on ocean governance is published in journals,[20] books,[21] and reports,[22] which frequently draw on multiple thematic and

Santos et al., "Integrating climate change in ocean planning," *Nature Sustainability* 3 (2020): 9, 505–16.

17 Ehler, Zaucha, and Gee, "Maritime/Marine Spatial Planning at the Interface of Research and Practice", 1; Michael Gilek, Fred Saunders, and Ignė Stalmokaitė, "The Ecosystem Approach and Sustainable Development in Baltic Sea Marine Spatial Planning: The Social Pillar, a 'Slow Train Coming'" in *The Ecosystem Approach in Ocean Planning and Governance*, ed. David Langlet and Rosemary Rayfuse (Leiden, Boston: BRILL, 2018): 160, 162; Jan-Gunnar Winther et al., "Integrated ocean management for a sustainable ocean economy," *Nature Ecology & Evolution* 4 (2020): 1451–58; Riku Varjopuro, "Evaluation of Marine Spatial Planning: Valuing the Process, Knowing the Impacts" in *Maritime Spatial Planning: Past, present, future*, ed. Jacek Zaucha and Kira Gee (Cham: Palgrave Macmillan, 2019): 417.

18 Pradeep Singh and Aline Jaeckel, "Future Prospects of Marine Environmental Governance," in *Handbook on Marine Environment Protection: Science, Impacts and Sustainable Management*, ed. Markus Salomon and Markus Till (Cham: Palgrave Macmillan, 2018): 621, 630.

19 For example, Erika Allen Wolters et al., "What is the best available science? A comparison of marine scientists, managers, and interest groups in the United States," *Ocean & coastal management* 122 (2016), 95–102, 98: "the only way to create sustainable marine policies is to have a formal regulatory instrument in place."

20 Such as *Marine Policy, Ocean and Coastal Management, Frontiers in Marine Science, ICES Journal of Marine Science, Ocean Development & International Law, The International Journal of Marine and Coastal Law, Maritime Studies, Ocean Yearbook, Oceanography, Tourism in Marine Environments, Western Indian Ocean Journal of Marine Science, Marine Biology Research*, and *African Journal of Marine Science*.

21 A few examples of book titles are *Routledge Handbook of Marine Governance and Global Environmental Change*; *Research Handbook on Climate Change, Oceans and Coasts*; *Handbook on Marine Environment Protection: Science, Impacts and Sustainable Management*; *Regime Interaction in Ocean Governance*; The Ecosystem Approach in Ocean Planning and Governance: Perspectives from Europe and Beyond; Comparative Ocean Governance: Place-based Protections in an Era of Climate Change; Sustainable Ocean Resource Governance: Deep Sea Mining, Marine Energy and Submarine Cables; Climate Change and Ocean Governance: Politics and Policy for Threatened Seas; Law, Science, and Ocean Management; Marine Ecology: Processes, Systems, and Impacts.

22 Several reports produced outside of traditional publishing and distribution channels, so-called gray literature, discuss ocean governance issues. Three examples of such reports

disciplinary perspectives.[23] These include governance perspectives such as governance,[24] management,[25] planning,[26] or policy.[27] Further, thematic and disciplinary perspectives include natural scientific or ecosystem scientific perspectives such as ocean or marine science,[28] marine ecology,[29] marine biology,[30]

---

that stand out in being authored by hundreds of scientists in renowned panels include H.-O. Pörtner et al., *IPCC 2019: Summary for Policymakers. In: IPCC Special Report on the Ocean and Cryosphere in a Changing Climate (IPCC special report), available at* https://www.ipcc.ch/srocc/ IPCC (Geneva, Switzerland, 2019), https://www.ipcc.ch/srocc/; Renison Ruwa et al., *The Second World Ocean Assessment—World Ocean Assessment II, available at* https://www.un.org/regularprocess/woa2launch (2021), https://www.un.org/regularprocess/woa2launch; and S. Díaz et al., *IPBES 2019: Summary for policymakers of the global assessment report on biodiversity and ecosystem services (summary for policy makers). IPBES Plenary at its seventh session (IPBES 7, Paris, 2019)*, IPBES (Bonn: Zenodo, 2019). On gray literature, also see Bertrum H. MacDonald et al., "Introduction," in *Science, information, and policy interface for effective coastal and ocean management*, ed. Bertrum H. MacDonald et al. (Boca Raton, Florida: CRC Press, 2016): 3, 5.

23 Similarly, as per Ehler, Zaucha, and Gee, "Maritime/Marine Spatial Planning at the Interface of Research and Practice." 2, "The imperative for employing a multidisciplinary approach stems from the nature of marine space as a multi-dimensional concept requiring insight from many scientific disciplines and types of knowledge."

24 For example, Bianca Haas et al., "The future of ocean governance," *Reviews in Fish Biology and Fisheries* (2021): 1–18.

25 For example, Markus Salomon and Till Markus, *Handbook on Marine Environment Protection: Science, Impacts and Sustainable Management* (Cham: Cham: Springer International Publishing, 2018).

26 For example, Santos et al., "Integrating climate change in ocean planning."

27 For example, Bueger, Christian, and Felix Mallin. "Blue Paradigms: Understanding the Intellectual Revolution in Global Ocean Politics." *International affairs* (London) 99, no. 4 (2023): 1719–39. Readers may note that the legal scholar may take 'policy' to mean those policies that are non-legally binding white papers and governmental plans and strategies (e.g. Katie Woolaston, *Ecological Vulnerability: The Law and Governance of Human–Wildlife Relationships* (Cambridge: Cambridge University Press, 2022), 11). The social scientist may perceive 'policies' as capturing both such policies and law (e.g. Carol Lee Bacchi, *Analysing policy: what's the problem represented to be?* (Frenchs Forest, NSW: Pearson Australia, 2009) and 'policy' as the research stream that in a wider sense concerns politics (e.g. Amitai Etzioni, "Introduction: Policy Research." *International Studies in Sociology and Social Anthropology*, vol. 26, (Leiden: Brill, 1978): 1–6. A list of examples of journals on public policy research: https://guides.library.ubc.ca/publicpolicy/journals).

28 For example, Vladimir Ryabinin et al., "The UN Decade of Ocean Science for Sustainable Development," Policy and Practice Reviews, *Frontiers in Marine Science* 6, no. 470 (2019): fmars.2019.00470.

29 For example, Michel J. Kaiser et al., *Marine ecology: processes, systems, and impacts*, Third edition. ed. (Oxford, England: Oxford University Press, 2020).

30 For example, André Monaco and Patrick Prouzet, *The Land-Sea Interactions*. Of *Oceanography and Marine Biology Series. Seas and Oceans Set.* (London: John Wiley & Sons, Incorporated, 2014).

and oceanography.[31] Furthermore, thematic and disciplinary perspectives include legal scientific perspectives including the law of the sea[32] and environmental law.[33] Thematic perspectives therefore capture the three knowledge domains of governance, science, and law.

The way in which the three knowledge domains are intertwined in the literature on ocean governance issues could further be illustrated by keyword searches of three key journals, reflecting different thematic approaches to ocean governance, namely *Marine Policy*, *ICES Journal of Marine Science*, and *Ocean Development & International Law*. These keyword searches find that multiple publications by all three journals refer to combinations of policy/governance, science, and law.[34] These results indicate that while each journal may focus on either policy/governance, science, or law, it is challenging to discuss ocean governance issues without stepping into the other domains.

This challenge begs for theory to increase the knowledge on the assumptions and presuppositions of governance, science, and law and their interfaces in ocean governance. Rich literature exists theorizing in general the relationship between science and society, under several frameworks such as the science–policy interface[35] or the more recent 'science of actionable knowledge'

---

31 For example, Teruhisa Komatsu et al., *Oceanography Challenges to Future Earth: Human and Natural Impacts on our Seas*, 1st 2019. ed. (Cham: Springer International Publishing: Imprint: Springer, 2019).

32 For example, Yoshinobu Takei, *A Sketch of the Concept of Ocean Governance and Its Relationship with the Law of the Sea*, ed. Cedric Ryngaert, Erik J. Molenaar, and Sarah M. H. Nouwen, vol. 27, Nova et Vetera Iuris Gentium, (2015): 48, 48.

33 For example, Elise Johansen, "The EU Influence on Norwegian Domestic Legislation for the Protection of the Arctic Marine Environment," *The International Journal of Marine and Coastal Law* 33, no. 2 (2018): 415–35.

34 Using the search tool of each of the journals' websites, *Marine Policy* had 1166 articles using all of the three terms 'governance,' 'science,' and 'law'; 2444 using 'governance'; 5899 using 'management'; 4157 using 'science'; 352 using 'science-based'; and 3924 using 'law.' The *ICES Journal of Marine Science* had no articles combining the three terms of 'governance,' 'science,' and 'law' but 2294 articles using the term 'governance'; 5183 using the term 'management'; and 1263 using the term 'law.' The *Ocean Development & International Law* journal had 501 articles using all the three terms 'governance,' 'science,' and 'law'; 888 using the term 'governance'; 785 using 'management'; 620 using 'science'; and 509 using 'science-based.' Searches conducted on 3 March 2023.

35 Roger A. Pielke, *The honest broker: making sense of science in policy and politics* (Cambridge: Cambridge University Press, 2007); Sheila Jasanoff, *States of Knowledge: The Co-Production of Science and the Social Order*, International library of sociology, (Abingdon, Oxon: Routledge, 2004); Sheila Jasanoff, *The fifth branch: Science advisers as policymakers* (Cambridge, Mass: Harvard University Press, 1990). Robert Hoppe, "Scientific advice and public policy: expert advisers' and policymakers' discourses on boundary work," *Poiesis & Praxis* 6, vol. 6 no. 3–4 (2009): 235–63.

(SOAK).[36] SOAK is an interdisciplinary area of inquiry aiming to build a nuanced and realistic understanding of "how science becomes actionable, that is, how science becomes used to inform decisions that enhance social and environmental well-being."[37] Jagannathan et al. catalogue systematically, by literature reviews and expert elicitations, assumptions on the science–policy interface and critical gaps in understanding of the science–society interface.[38] They assert that, "[d]ue to its centrality, we conclude our paper by raising questions about the generative potential of using governance as a lens for future studies of SOAK."[39] This study precisely uses governance as a lens to investigate what is therefore the governance–science relationship, and, additionally, the governance–law relationship.

SOAK and science–policy interface literature repeatedly highlights how science–policy interfaces are highly contextual.[40] In the context of ocean governance, the governance–science and the governance–law interfaces are less theorized.[41] One exception is MacDonald et al., discussing the science, information, and policy interface for effective coastal and ocean management.[42] Some other exceptions are Boesch discussing the role of science in ocean governance,[43] and Rudd analyzing scientists' framing of the ocean science–policy interface.[44] The lack of theorizing leaves open questions such as what ocean governance is, various ways in which and the extent to which (marine) science can inform governance, and different ways in which law relates to governance. The advantages of theorizing these relationships in a relatively limited (ocean) context is that the variables become fewer, the study may draw on practical

36 Kripa Jagannathan et al., "A research agenda for the science of actionable knowledge: Drawing from a review of the most misguided to the most enlightened claims in the science-policy interface literature," *Environmental science & policy* 144 (2023): 174–86.

37 Ibid, 175.

38 Ibid.

39 Ibid, 181.

40 For example, Jagannathan et al., "A research agenda for the science of actionable knowledge: Drawing from a review of the most misguided to the most enlightened claims in the science-policy interface literature," 180 and 181, and Pielke, *The honest broker: making sense of science in policy and politics*, 136.

41 Unlike, investigating by empirical work and case studies, such as McConney et al., "A First Look at the Science-Policy Interface for Ocean Governance in the Wider Caribbean Region."

42 MacDonald et al., "Introduction," 4.

43 Donald F. Boesch, "The role of science in ocean governance," *Ecological economics* 31, no. 2 (1999): 189–198.

44 Murray A. Rudd, "Scientists' framing of the ocean science–policy interface," *Global environmental change* 33 (2015): 44–60.

examples from a familiar context, and the generalizations become less overall compared with if the study also accounted for governance of properties, health scientific input, and criminal legal principles.[45] Further, the ocean governance context provides for the development of an approach to governance extending beyond generalizable components of generic governance, such as structures and processes or a system. Nonetheless, the ocean governance context could also be perceived as broad, leading to generalizations and simplification within the context.

1.2 *Method and Approach*

The method of this study is theorizing, which essentially means exploring, systematizing, and discussing, by thinking, writing, and engaging with relevant literature and governance instruments (policies and regulation). Relevant for legal discourse and beyond, Twining states how theorizing:

> has several functions or 'jobs': constructing total pictures (synthesising); clarification and construction of individual concepts and conceptual frameworks; (…) and so on—wherever thinking at a relatively general level contributes to understanding.[46]

Similarly, this study essentially thinks about ocean governance at a relatively general level by constructing and synthesizing, or conceptualizing, a perspective on governance. This perspective systematizes and divides governance into three basic subsets or components: structures and processes; ideals and

45 While theorizing these topics may certainly enrich science and society, the capacity of each study is limited.

46 William Twining, *Jurist in Context: A Memoir* (Cambridge: Cambridge University Press, 2019): 5. By introducing Twining, this research owes it to specify some inherent assumptions articulated by Twining that it does not challenge but rather, to some extent, relies on: "a. that law consists of two principal kinds of ordering: municipal state law and public international law (classically conceived as ordering the relations between states) ('the Westphalian duo'); b. that nation-states, societies, and legal systems are very largely closed, self-contained entities that can be studied in isolation; (…) d. that modern state law is primarily rational–bureaucratic and instrumental, performing certain functions and serving as a means for achieving particular social ends; e. that law is best understood through 'top-down' perspectives of rulers, officials, legislators and elites with the points of view of users, consumers, victims and other subjects being at best marginal (…)," p. 251. This research argues for pluralistic views, leaving research space to explore, for example, both deep assumptions and subsurface assumptions, both 'top-down' perspectives, 'bottom-up' perspectives, and other perspectives diverging from vertical logic.

standards; and substance or merits.[47] The reason for choosing these components is twofold, first, to focus on these components reflects an aim to capture components which are often referred to in the ocean governance literature: coordination, participatory processes, science-based decision-making, adaptivity or responsiveness, and the ecosystem approach[48] thereby aiming to develop a suitable framework into which these components could belong and be analyzed.

Second, dividing governance into these components provides a basis for clarification and refinement of these governance components and for discussing and nuancing the relationships of these components with science and law. While the approach could seem too categorical or rational, the rationality aimed for by the approach of this study is, as per Kooiman, that which is "methodical and precise, as tidy and orderly, above all in thought, (…)" an approach that "separates all separable issues and deals with them one at a time (…) to avoid muddling up issues."[49] Identifying separable components of governance and dealing with them one at a time to avoid muddling up issues is a key driver of this study. For this reason, this study does not approach ocean governance through the lens of concepts or ideals often associated with ocean governance (such as, integrated management, ecosystem approach, marine spatial planning).[50] These concepts frequently combine elements of governance, science, and, more implicitly, law in ways that would challenge investigating the separable components of governance, science, and law.

---

47 Studies focusing on the 'realities' of ocean governance are rarer, Peter J. S. Jones, L. M. Lieberknecht, and W. Qiu, "Marine spatial planning in reality: Introduction to case studies and discussion of findings," *Marine Policy* 71 (2016): 256–64.

48 See notes 18–22 for examples of such references. As per David Langlet and Rosemary Rayfuse, "The Ecosystem Approach in Ocean Planning and Governance: An Introduction," in *The Ecosystem Approach in Ocean Planning and Governance*, ed. David Langlet and Rosemary Rayfuse, Perspectives from Europe and Beyond (Leiden: BRILL, 2019): 1, the ecosystem approach "has come to feature particularly strongly in the context of marine management," 2. In searches of three journals covering ocean governance issues (*Marine Policy*, *ICES Journal of Marine Science*, and *Ocean Development & International Law*), the journals' search tools returned 1525, 1315, and 467 hits, respectively, for 'coordination'; 921, 37, and 589 hits for 'participatory process'; 352, 138, and 508 hits for 'science-based'; 2455, 2985, and 234 hits for 'adaptivity OR adaptive'; and 3109, 3147, and 244 hits for 'ecosystem approach.' The searches were conducted on January 9 and February 2, 2023. Readers may note that while these searches indicate a pattern, these keywords are not only used in the context or meaning that this study attaches to them.

49 Jan Kooiman, *Governing as Governance* (London: SAGE Publications, 2003), 173.

50 Robert L. Stephenson et al., "The Quilt of Sustainable Ocean Governance: Patterns for Practitioners," *Frontiers in Marine Science* 8 (2021): 630547, 2.

Another key assumption of this study is the necessity of plural perspectives complementing each other in terms of abstraction level and which connections or components they focus on (while this study only captures one). As put by Meadows and Wright departing from a system perspective:

> I don't think a systems way of seeing is better than the reductionist way of thinking. I think it's complementary, and therefore revealing. You can see some things through the lens of the human eye, other things through the lens of a microscope, others through the lens of a telescope, and still others through the lens of systems theory. Everything seen through each kind of lens is actually there. Each way of seeing allows our knowledge of the wondrous world in which we live to become a little more complete.[51]

The necessity of different perspectives further reflects, as per Davies, "current intellectual preference, in favor of plural explanations (complexity, diversity, deconstruction)."[52] A consequence of this belief in plurality is that limitations are inherent in any perspective. Since any perspective is limited, it should therefore be justified and the limits highlighted.

While the three-components governance perspective of this study is limited, it does offer criteria and a method that facilitates distinguishing between the structure and processes, the ideals and standards, and the substance or merit of an area of governance. In this sense, the governance perspective is analytically generalizable.[53] For example, one could imagine employing the same set of criteria to analyze other concepts or areas of governance (as will briefly be shown with the ecosystem approach in section 5.1.3). Nonetheless, this study has a marine focus in the examples provided and in the literature it relates to. The vastness and multiform nature of the literature discussing ocean governance entail that this study occasionally attributes to this scholarship that which is 'often' or 'frequently' addressed there. Exceptions exist and should be expected. Although the approach sometimes refers to generic governance, the study is written from a technocratic Western science perspective and may not reflect realities and contexts elsewhere.

---

51 Donella H. Meadows and Diana Wright, *Thinking in systems: a primer* (White River Junction, Vermont: Earthscan, 2009), 7.

52 Margaret Davies, "Theoretical Variables" in *Law Unlimited: Materialism, Pluralism and Legal Theory*, ed. Margaret Davies (London: Taylor and Francis, 2017): 1, 11.

53 Lise Justesen and Nanna Mik-Meyer, *Qualitative research methods in organisation studies* (Copenhagen: Hans Reitzels Forl., 2012), 42; Robert K. Yin, *Case study research and applications: design and methods*, 6th ed. (Los Angeles: SAGE, 2018), 45.

The governance perspective dominates this study. Thus, the roles and relevance of 'science' and 'law' are determined by their relevance to the governance perspective in an ocean governance context. Science and law certainly have roles and relevance beyond the approach undertaken. The law–science interface could immediately appear outside the scope of this study. However, the study will show how law is embedded in, and key to, governance and will investigate the governance–science interface. Thus, the law–science interface is covered indirectly by the approach.

Having introduced governance (section 2.1) and separated separable components of governance (section 2.2–2.4), this study clarifies and refines the relationships between governance and science (section 3), after introducing science (section 3.1) by discussing the relevance of science to governance structures and processes (section 3.2), the ideals and standards of governance (section 3.3), and the substance of governance (section 3.4). Further, this study refines the relationship between governance and law (section 4), after introducing law (section 4.1) by discussing the relevance of law to governance structures and processes (section 4.2), ideals and standards of governance (section 4.3), and the substance of governance (section 4.4). Finally, based on these sections, the study provides some perspectives on some ideals and standards common to ocean governance that traverses the science–policy interface (section 5.1) and draws conclusions on the study (section 5.2).

2 A Governance Perspective

2.1 *Introduction to Governance*

The concept of 'governance' semantically refers to the act of governing[54] and often embraces the complexity of human interaction. The concept is used in several ways depending on the theoretical and practical context.[55] In the ocean governance context, the term 'governance' conveniently highlights the social (human) aspects of ocean research and practice (albeit embedded in ecosystems).

---

54 WordNet 3.0, Farlex clipart collection. S.v. "governance." Retrieved 1 November 2023 from https://www.thefreedictionary.com/governance.

55 R. A. W. Rhodes, "Understanding Governance: Ten Years On," *Organization studies* 28, no. 8 (2007): 1243–64; Kooiman, *Governing as Governance*; Aurelia Colombi Ciacchi and Dietmar von der Pfordten, "Exploring the relationship between law and governance: a proposal," *The Theory and Practice of Legislation* 11, no. 2 (2023): 151–67.

Inspired by the classic works on governance of Kooiman and Rhodes,[56] this study defines governance as the collective structures and processes, ideals and standards, interactions and actions, of humans, aimed at solving societal problems or creating societal opportunities, inside and outside of institutions and organizations, such as states, other public actors, private actors, and non-state organizations.[57] Similar to most definitions of governance,[58] this one is inclusive and covers a multifaceted reality.[59] Any study of such intricate reality will only shed light on certain aspects or components, which is why this study focuses on three selected components of governance.

Resorting to definitions (as per this section) and components (as per the subsequent sections 2.2 to 2.4) is but one way of approaching governance. To highlight the diversity of potential approaches to governance, of which this study only captures one, some other governance approaches will briefly be introduced. Some approach governance as an umbrella concept which encompasses some key components or themes, such as Kooiman and Bavinck's actors,

---

56 Kooiman, *Governing as Governance*; Rhodes, "Understanding Governance: Ten Years On."

57 Three other definitions are: "a social function centered on efforts to steer or guide the actions of human groups—from small local associations to international society—toward the achievement of desired ends," in Oran R Young, *On environmental governance: Sustainability, efficiency, and equity* (New York: Routledge, 2016): 3 and "purposeful and authoritative steering of societal processes by political actors. Governance thus includes traditional activities by governance actors, such as laws, policies, and regulations; planning practices, rule systems, and procedures at subnational levels; and certain actions by nongovernmental actors, such as standards set by civil society networks or public-private partnerships, as long as these activities include a claim to authority, have some legitimacy, and are designed to steer behaviour. While there are some debates in the literature regarding the exact boundaries of what counts as governance, there is general agreement that authority and steering are its two core components," in Frank Biermann et al., "Global Goal Setting for Improving National Governance and Policy," in *Governing through Goals*, ed. Frank Biermann and Norichika Kanie, Sustainable Development Goals as Governance Innovation (The MIT Press, 2017): 75, 75.

58 For example, Rhodes, "Understanding Governance: Ten Years On;" Biermann et al., "Global Goal Setting for Improving National Governance and Policy;" Young, *On environmental governance: Sustainability, efficiency, and equity*.

59 In comparison, approaches to management (such as public management or resource management) may be less inclusive or simpler, as in referring to the steering only by public actors (public management) or to the administration only of one or more resources (resource management). Inherent in management approaches could be a limited set of roles, including managing subjects or a hierarchy. In comparison, the governance frame, capturing interaction and multiple actors at multiple levels, involves a broader range of actors that may have dissimilar roles in different relations. Nonetheless, either term may be defined for a given purpose and given a content as seen fit.

institutions, principles, and interactions of,[60] or Armstrong and Kilpatrick's actors; tools or instruments; modes or attributes; and architecture.[61] Yet others approach governance as a system, which could attract a system-theoretical approach, premised on interpretations of complexity theory.[62]

Since system-theoretical approaches are popular and sometimes dominant in the current governance discourse across disciplines, including the discourse on ocean governance,[63] the governance approach of this study will be aligned with some approaches to the 'adaptive governance' frame, which is closely related to system-theoretical perspectives.[64] The approach of this study is framed as governance, rather than adaptive governance, yet it deals with responsiveness or adaptivity as one of the process phases of governance and discusses the adaptability inherent in the fundamental design of governance instruments.

As is the case with governance, 'adaptive governance' is also used in several ways.[65] Adaptive governance is, for example, defined as "governance that

---

60 Jan Kooiman and Maarten Bavinck, "The Governance Perspective," in *Fish for Life: Interactive Governance for Fisheries*, ed. Jan Kooiman et al. (Amsterdam University Press, 2005): 15–17.

61 Kenneth Kilpatrick Armstrong, Claire, "Law, Governance, or New Governance—The Changing Open Method of Coordination Narrowing the Gap: Law and New Approaches to Governance in the European Union," *Colum. J. Eur. L.* 13 (2006): 652–655. The listed themes are those that these authors conceptualize as 'new governance,' which includes the theme 'new governance as not-old governance.'

62 Stephenson et al., "The Quilt of Sustainable Ocean Governance: Patterns for Practitioners," 1, Identifies a social-ecological systems approach as a key concept to managing marine activities. System-theoretical perspectives include different schools of thought. Some focus on socioecological systems, closely related to resilience thinking. Others focus on sociotechnical regimes that have emerged from evolutionary economics, science/technology and society studies, and innovations research. Some combine these into socio–ecological–technological systems. All these systems perspectives are premised on interpretations of complexity theory. See Tanya Brodie Rudolph et al., "A transition to sustainable ocean governance," *Nature Communications* 11, no. 1 (2020): 3600 and Cosens et al., "Governing complexity: Integrating science, governance, and law to manage accelerating in the commons.". Stephenson et al., "The Quilt of Sustainable Ocean Governance: Patterns for Practitioners."

63 Stephenson et al., "The Quilt of Sustainable Ocean Governance: Patterns for Practitioners," 1.

64 J. B. Ruhl, Barbara Cosens, and Niko Soininen, "Resilience of Legal Systems: Toward Adaptive Governance," in *Multisystemic Resilience*, ed. Michael Ungar (New York: Oxford Academic, 2021): 509, 521.

65 Thomas Dietz, Elinor Ostrom, and Paul C. Stern, "The Struggle to Govern the Commons," *Science* 302, no. 5652 (2003): 1907–12, were the first to introduce the term, focusing on the struggle of institutional complexity and design. Lyndal Hasselman, "Adaptive management; adaptive co-management; adaptive governance: what's the difference?," *Australasian Journal of Environmental Management* 24, no. 1 (2017): 31–46 compares different

allows emergence of collective action capable of facilitating adaptation to change and surprise as well as the capacity itself to evolve."[66] Further, adaptive governance promotes the "adaptive capacity at the macro-scale of social-ecological systems."[67] Some key attributes of complex systems relevant to governance are self-organization, emergence, networks, feedback, nonlinearity and tipping points, and uncertainty.[68] These definitions, characteristics, and attributes reflect how system theorists may focus on the dynamism of a system (as in interaction, flux, and emergence), unpredictability (as in change, surprise, uncertainty), and a multiplicity of attributes, perhaps reflecting its roots in complexity theory.

In contrast to dynamism, unpredictability, complexity, and adaptivity at system level, this study approaches governance, within a limited context, as a set of three components: structures and processes; ideals or standards; and substance or merit, which the following sub-sections will unpack. Some system theorists hold that any system can be defined by its structure and processes,[69] which capture some of the governance components of this study. The chosen governance perspective could be critiqued for being too categorical, simple, or relying on a mechanical worldview. Yet, as per Kooiman:

> [g]overning has in some way to be rational (...) Rationality in governing thus means the acceptance of certain degrees of uncertainties, the realisation of partial knowledge and provisional insights, and learning by doing.[70]

Thus, this study aims to balance the focus on rationality with awareness of, and by highlighting, the partial knowledge, simplicity, limitations, and risk of uncertainty inherent in any approach including this one.

---

approaches to 'adaptive governance'. Hasselman explains how the "relationship of adaptive governance to governance is also questionable, with adaptive governance defined variously as a mode of governance and as a quality of good governance," 39.

66 Ruhl, Cosens, and Soininen, "Resilience of Legal Systems: Toward Adaptive Governance," 522 (referring to Cosens 2018).

67 Ibid, 523.

68 Cosens et al., "Governing complexity: Integrating science, governance, and law to manage accelerating in the commons," 4.

69 Ruhl, Cosens, and Soininen, "Resilience of Legal Systems: Toward Adaptive Governance," 512.

70 Kooiman, *Governing as Governance*, 172.

2.2 *Structures and Processes of Governance*

2.2.1 Governance Structures

This section approaches governance as taking place within a structure within which (time-bound) policy-making, law-making, and decision-making processes take place.[71] The governance structure captures institutions and organizational units (such as states, other public actors, private actors, and non-state organizations) that include actors such as politicians, bureaucrats, or stakeholders. Therefore, the approach of this section to the governance structures, and the units within these structures, is deliberately simple to emphasize the analytical and logical limits inherent in any governance structures. Different approaches to governance structures and units that expands on the level of complexity, or layers of context include the regime lens, which captures functional issue-areas including institutions and beyond (e.g., behavior, assumptions, biases).[72]

Public or international and regional institutions and organizational entities often have a mandate delegated to them by one or more states. For nongovernmental institutions and organizations, the specific mandate of each of them would be recorded in statutes or other foundational documents. Each mandate of a state, substate unit, an organization, or other unit is limited and, accordingly, a partition. Partition of governance structures in units reflects current governance realities, where governance takes place in and across multiple institutions and organizations (such as states, substate units, and regional organizations, forming one or several structures). One example is the Australian Maritime Safety Authority, which is "Australia's national agency responsible for maritime safety, protection of the marine environment, and maritime aviation search and rescue,"[73] which is under the Ministry for Infrastructure, Transport, Regional Development, Communications, and the Arts of the Australian government. Another example is the Arctic Council, an intergovernmental forum of eight Arctic member states, participants, and observers, which provides a

---

71 This subsection is inspired by Lena Schøning, "A Critical Assessment of the Contribution of Integrated Ocean Management to Protection of the Marine Environment" (PhD Diss., UiT The Arctic University of Norway, 2021).

72 Margaret A. Young, "Regime Interaction in Creating, Implementing and Enforcing International Law," in *Regime Interaction in International Law: Facing Fragmentation*, ed. Margaret A. Young (Cambridge: Cambridge University Press, 2012), 86.

73 Source: https://www.amsa.gov.au/about/who-we-are#collapseArea177 (last accessed 25 April 2023)

means for promoting cooperation, coordination, and interaction, overseeing six working groups, and disseminating information.[74]

From the perspective that explains the current partition or division of governance structures, such as from an Australian perspective on maritime issues (including maritime safety, marine environmental protection, and maritime rescue) in the aforementioned example, the approach is holistic or integrated. But from another perspective, such as that of protection of nature, the perspective only captures the marine environment. From the perspective of the safety of fisheries, approaching maritime safety in general may not account for the particular concerns for the safety of fishing vessels. Both of these perspectives may challenge the Australian perspective on maritime issues as fragmented.

Another classic example of fragmentation may be provided. In a structure divided by activity type or sector—a sectorally divided structure—the approach could be holistic or integrated from the sectoral point of view, such as in governing the life cycle of fisheries in the fisheries sector. From the perspective that does not reflect such a division, such as managing the multiuse of fisheries and other marine sectors or managing the climate gas emissions stemming from all kinds of marine activities, the governance structure is 'fragmented' across multiple (sectoral) divisions. Thus, some topics or perspectives will always be governed across other divisions, topics, or perspectives or be governed in a 'fragmented' way, since no perspective could focus both on the commonalities of maritime sectors and the specifics of each sector. No partition or division would account for all of the different perspectives that governance demands. Therefore, inherent in any governance structure partitioned into units is a risk of fragmentation, fragmentation is logically speaking unavoidable, thus one cannot reorganize away from fragmentation.

Nonetheless, statements framing fragmentation as an avoidable problem are frequent in ocean governance literature. Agardy, for example, has observed:

> Like many other assessments and publications before and since, the 2006 National Academy of Sciences book entitled *Increasing Capacity Building for Stewardship of Oceans and Coasts: A Priority for the 21st Century* (NRC, 2006) identified fragmentation of management as one of the most pervasive and prominent obstacles to effective marine management. Ocean zoning by its very nature overcomes fragmentation—obligating

---

74 Article 1 of the Declaration on the establishment of the Arctic Council (Ottawa Declaration), (1996). http://hdl.handle.net/11374/85.

> the managers of all the various sectors using marine resources and ocean space to think strategically and plan for sustainable use.[75]

While ocean zoning may overcome some issues of fragmentation, it may further increase the risk of fragmentation of, for example, the holistic management of each sector.

This inherent risk of fragmentation exists both within the structure to which a governance unit belongs and in relation to other units with similar or overlapping mandates. In the example of the Australian Maritime Safety Authority, its governing in accordance with its mandate to protect the marine environment risks being poorly coordinated with or lacking interaction with, for example, the Ministry of Agriculture, Water, and the Environment which also has a mandate involving capturing environmental issues as well as with other units of the nation state of Australia. Further, the governing of Australia to protect the marine environment, including by the Australian Maritime Safety Authority, risks being poorly coordinated with or lacking interaction with similar efforts of neighboring and other states, private actors, and organizations.

While partition of governance into units may be unavoidable (for example, to preserve manageable units), how to partition is more complicated. For a simplified example, a state may distribute its mandate over ocean governance issues to a ministry of trade and industry, a ministry of the environment, a ministry of oceans, or partition it between two or more of these, reflecting, for example, how ocean governance is perceived as the management of maritime industries, the protection and preservation of the marine environment, both, or something else. Another example, sectoral division of activities and management by a state, such as separating fisheries management from offshore petroleum production, may be suitable for the level of detail and expertise expected in the allocation of licenses to fishers and petroleum companies, yet may be less suitable for coordinating fisheries and offshore petroleum activities in time and space.

In documents and textual expressions, such as in a research paper or in a policy, plural alternative, crosscutting, diverging, or conflicting perspectives can be envisioned to accommodate the limits inherent in each partitioning or perspective. Therefore, we may have policies, plans, and strategies that address planning of, for example, the multiuse of marine space by different sectors which cuts across sectoral divisions. We may have topical laws and policies that address an environmental problem, such as climate change or pollution, across all sectors and activities. Regulations or policies addressing particular

75 Agardy, *Ocean Zoning: Making Marine Management More Effective*, 6.

resources (such as water) may also cross-cut sectoral mandates.[76] In institutional and organizational realities, however, plural ways of partitioning may conflict with concerns for structural integration (such as a hierarchy) and concerns for streamlined and efficient institutions and organizations.

"Streamlined and efficient" institutions or organizations could refer to the capacity of these of being simple and cost-effective, for example by reduction of bureaucracy and avoiding overlapping mandates. For example, a state may wish to delegate power and organize institutions according to one perspective only (such as the logic of sectoral division or the logic of one ocean ministry). Or the High Seas Biodiversity Treaty that seeks to establish institutions without undermining existing institutions.[77] In contrast, plural crosscutting, diverging, or conflicting mandates in an institution or organization could compromise the streamlined and efficient structure. While institutions with crosscutting mandates may of course contribute to cooperation and strengthened efforts, it may also lead to double work, confusion of who does what, and the pulling in different directions.

While partitioning is one perspective on governance structures, interconnectedness is another. No institution or organization (whether a state, regional organization, or substate unit) exists in a vacuum but rather in a structure or 'family' of parent units, sibling units, grandchildren units and beyond, as well as units with competing or conflicting purposes whether within or outside the same 'family' structure.

Ways of preventing fragmentation structurally, within or outside, the 'family' structure, include facilitating consultation, coordination, cooperation, or structural integration between the units, which reflects various ways of enhancing structural integration.[78] The Australian Maritime Safety Authority may need to cooperate on marine environmental matters with the Ministry of Agriculture, Water and the Environment and coordinate safety matters with maritime safety authorities of other nations while consulting the International Maritime Organization. The Arctic Council formalized its cooperation with Convention for the Protection of the Marine Environment of the North-East Atlantic Commission (OSPAR) in 2017 by making OSPAR an observer to the

---

76 Lena Schøning, Vera Helene Hausner, and Mathilde Morel, "Law and sustainable transitions: An analysis of aquaculture regulation," *Environmental Innovation and Societal Transitions* 48 (2023): 100753, 2.

77 "Agreement under the United Nations Convention on the Law of the Sea on the conservation and sustainable use of marine biological diversity of areas beyond national jurisdiction, adopted 19 June 2023." art. 5 (2) and 22 (2).

78 Schøning, "A Critical Assessment of the Contribution of Integrated Ocean Management to Protection of the Marine Environment," 38.

Arctic Council, which is one way of preventing fragmentation structurally.[79] Organizing a structure hierarchically, under common instruction or leadership, provides another way to prevent fragmentation structurally. For instance, in a nation state, all sectoral governance units are organized hierarchically under the head of state or government, entailing that it is a cross-sectoral authority that may approach matters in a cross-sectoral way, for example, based on instructional authority.

At the international level, structural integration in terms of a hierarchy is less relevant for the 200 or so states and the regional and international organizations made by these. Nonetheless, size, geographic position, geopolitics, military power, alliances, common interests, and trade may connect or integrate some more than others through unions, alliances, and institutions. Preventing fragmentation between such units may also be made by consultation, coordination, or cooperation.

In any event, fragmentation remains unavoidable and an inherent risk of any governance structure, reflecting how institutions and organizations, and associated mandates, are multiple units or partitions of the greater governance whole. Fragmentation reflects partitioning for a purpose that may be less appropriate for other purposes. The extent to which partitioning is a problem arguably demands justification as it depends on the purpose of partition. Therefore, the approach to governance structures of this study will investigate the relevance of science and law to the partitioning into units, the risks of fragmentation, and ways of preventing fragmentation.

2.2.2 Governance Processes

As per this study, governance processes or management processes (these terms are used interchangeably) are the time-bound actions that take place within or across governance structures, such as policy-making, law-making, and decision-making processes. Although management processes are as old as management, they have received a stronger focus in recent decades.[80]

This study approaches these processes in a stepwise manner, as phases.[81] A simplified account of the phases includes the following: knowledge gathering

---

79 The Arctic Council describes this cooperation on its webpages, source: https://www.ospar.org/about/international-cooperation/the-arctic-council (last accessed 23 April 2023).

80 Johan Quist and Andreas Hellström, "Process Management as a Contagious Idea: A Contribution to Røvik's Virus-Inspired Theory," *International Journal of Public Administration* 35, no. 13 (2012): 901–13, 902.

81 MacDonald et al., *Science, information, and policy interface for effective coastal and ocean management*, 67, explains how the stages model of the governance process has been described and criticized in the literature.

and analysis; policy- and decision-making with regard to objectives and priorities, and tools and strategies; implementation and monitoring; and evaluation and adaptation.[82] Individual management processes could sometimes be cyclic and iterative, such as that of adopting a policy (policy cycles), if the topic is a recurring topic, such as maritime safety.[83] However, policies for new or reframed topics, such as blue economy[84] or marine plastic pollution,[85] may not be cyclic or iterative, but rather examples of new layers of policy adopted by linear processes. Furthermore, regulations such as statutory acts or treaties would be adopted by an individual management process that are normally not cyclic or iterative in the sense that acts and treaties are commonly not up for regular revision.[86] However, such regulations may provide for other management processes, whether by mandating authority to make decisions, such as to protect

82 For a simplified but essentially similar explanation of the management process for organizations, see Stuart Winby and Christopher G. Worley, "Management processes for agility, speed, and innovation," *Organizational Dynamics* 43, no. 3 (2014): 225–34. For corporate management processes, see, for example, Richard Lynch, *Corporate strategy*, 2nd ed. (Harlow: Financial Times, 2000), 26. For similar but more extensive representations of management processes for marine spatial planning, see Vanessa Stelzenmüller et al., "Monitoring and evaluation of spatially managed areas: A generic framework for implementation of ecosystem based marine management and its application," *Marine Policy* 37 (2013): 149–64. See also the Monitoring and Evaluation of Spatially Managed Areas project, which addresses management processes relevant to marine spatial planning, including an evaluation framework: https://maritime-spatial-planning.ec.europa.eu/projects/monitoring-and-evaluation-spatially-managed-areas (last accessed 4 November 2023).

83 For example, EU is currently revising its maritime security policy, source: https://transport.ec.europa.eu/news-events/news/maritime-safety-new-proposals-support-clean-and-modern-shipping-2023-06-01_en (last accessed 4 November 2023).

84 India is, for example, finalizing its first blue economy policy, as per a press release, source: https://pib.gov.in/PressReleasePage.aspx?PRID=1845257 (last accessed 4 November 2023). Norway did, for example, develop its first program on marine litter and microplastics in 2018, as per the government, source: https://www.regjeringen.no/en/dokumenter/marine_litter/id2642037/ (last accessed 4 November 2023).

85 Examples of marine plastic pollution policies, see F. Alpizar et al., "A framework for selecting and designing policies to reduce marine plastic pollution in developing countries," *Environmental Science & Policy* 109 (2020): 25–35.

86 Which is why, for example, some legal texts remain unrevised, such as treaties like UNCLOS or the Convention on Biological Diversity (CBD), adopted June 5, 1992, entered into force 29 December 1993, 1760 UNTS 79. A (national) statutory act like, for example, the Norwegian pollution act of 1981, is not up for regular revision, but has been revised on several occasions to reflect, for example, gender neutral terminology, stricter sanctions and beyond.

marine areas or to grant licenses to pollute or emit, or to issue detailed regulations, guidelines, or recommendations.[87]

An individual management process coexists with multiple other processes, and one may envision that management processes concerning related topics could be combined or integrated, insofar as procedural requirements and institutional diversity allow. For example, one could imagine that a multiuse coastal zone planning process was suggested to be combined with or coordinated with the decision-making processes of granting licenses to aquaculture farms. While these processes may have some overlap in their mandate, the institutions carrying out the processes (such as a municipality or an aquaculture authority), the competence they require, and the legal requirements to the processes (including who shall be involved and how) may differ. While some coordination may be possible, such as in the mandates and in consulting across the processes, limits exist on the potential to integrate governance processes.

MacDonald et al. separate linear and cyclical governance processes reflecting stepwise progression between identifiable points from dynamic, interactive, and multidimensional models that take a system-theoretical approach.[88] This study approaches the governance processes in a simpler way, where the process is treated as individual and linear, where each of the phases are elaborated to facilitate investigating the relationship with science and law. In reality, the management processes may often be less tidy, as legal requirements may demand the use of specific measures or instructions from superior bodies may indicate preferred outcomes, leaving less space for upfront analysis and consideration of alternatives. Criticism of approaching stepwise progression of management processes also exists, including how science "usually affects the development and modification of policy in diffuse ways. It provides a background of empirical generalizations and ideas that *creep* into policy deliberations."[89] However, as section 4 will unpack, the "diffuse ways" that science creep into policy deliberations may be unpacked and clarified, to some extent. Pahl-Wostl describes how the policy phases, who she sees as cyclical, could lead to and be complemented by cyclical learning processes of reframing, which could

87 For example, building on the examples of the previous footnote, art 23 of the CBD establishes a process of conference of parties that makes recommendations on biodiversity matters, and chapter 3 of the Norwegian pollution act establishes a process of licensing pollution emissions.

88 MacDonald et al., "Understanding the Science–Policy Interface in Integrated Coastal and Ocean Management," 55–57.

89 Carol H. Weiss, "Knowledge Creep and Decision Accretion," *Knowledge* 1, no. 3 (1980): 381–404, 381.

again support learning cycles of transformation.[90] In alignment, the approach to the governance process phases of this study will capture the frame of reference and the importance of guiding assumption as part of the process phases, while the transformation of the structural constraints is out-of-scope.[91]

The study will now provide a brief account of the phases of an ideal linear management process, starting with the knowledge gathering and analysis phase. On the one hand, the knowledge gathering and analysis phase, in providing for collection of facts and knowledge (which section 3 spells out in more detail) and ensuring that considerations come before decisions, may be perceived as wide or open. On the other hand, the knowledge and facts gathered represent, whether implicitly or explicitly, a selection of knowledge and a focus of analyses, which frame and may strongly influence subsequent policies and decisions. Policies and laws not only react to problems but create, frame, and define problems, which sets the premises for the voices heard and the responses considered.[92] In ocean governance, policies and regulation (and associated decisions) could be pursuing many and complex societal objectives and problems concurrently, especially if the mandate is broad or vague, as may be the case for integrated marine management plans or marine spatial plans. The selection of knowledge and choice of foci in such instruments would be complicated to make, to justify, and to foresee the consequences for the remaining process. For example, the focus of such plans could be on the co-existence of local activities in space and time, or it could be how to protect the marine environment of the area in question.[93] The former could focus on local activities, while the latter could focus on the main global threat to the marine environmental problems of

90 Claudia Pahl-Wostl, "A conceptual framework for analysing adaptive capacity and multi-level learning processes in resource governance regimes," *Global Environmental Change* 19, no. 3 (2009): 354–65, and similar Cosens et al., "Governing complexity: Integrating science, governance, and law to manage accelerating in the commons," 7.

91 Pahl-Wostl, "A conceptual framework for analysing adaptive capacity and multi-level learning processes in resource governance regimes," 359.

92 Carol Bacchi and Susan Goodwin, "Making and Unmaking 'problems'," in *Poststructural Policy Analysis: A Guide to Practice*, ed. Carol Bacchi and Susan Goodwin (New York: Palgrave Macmillan US, 2016): 57.

93 Lena Schøning, "The Contribution of Integrated Marine Policies to Marine Environmental Protection: The Case of Norway," *The International Journal of Marine and Coastal Law* (2021): 263–93.

increased demand for space.[94] Thus, the framing could facilitate quite different directions to the plan.

If a policy or regulation (or associated decision) has a more focused purpose, such as preparing for a new statutory act on sustainable seabed mining, implicit choices could still be envisioned in the initial phase. Does the knowledge gathering and analysis phase leave open whether to facilitate seabed mining or to pursue other alternatives such as to search for alternative minerals elsewhere, expanding existing mines, or banning seabed mining, or is this principal decision implicit as the process is initiated? To whom will the act bring benefits and to whom disadvantages?[95] In any event, the process may be imagined going back and forth from the next phase—the policy- and decision-making phase—to be reframed and provide for new selections of knowledge and demanding new analyses, when the consequences of implied choices realize.

The next phase is the policy- and decision-making phase. It is where a maritime policy or fisheries regulation is adopted or where decisions such as the emission permit or licensing or restriction of activities in a marine space are decided. These adoptions and decisions pursue or prioritize certain societal objectives and may make use of certain tools or strategies to pursue them, thus deselecting other objectives and strategies. The more complex the objectives and priorities, the more is demanded of selection and choices of focus, which is preferably explicated in a transparent manner. Section 2.4 on the substance of governance instruments will elaborate on ways of designing and evaluating the substance of governance instruments.

The subsequent phase is the implementation and monitoring phase. Implementation could refer to when the policy or regulation on paper is put into practice administratively. A newly adopted policy or regulation may require institutional changes, measures to be initiated, decisions to be made, financial allocations, further regulations to be made or revised, licenses or permits to be issued, or new connections or ideas to be accounted for. One often implicit assumption of implementation is that it is uniformly carried out by different implementers assuming the policy, regulation, or decision to be implemented is clear, unambiguous, noncontradictory, and not asking

---

94 Díaz et al., *IPBES 2019: Summary for policymakers of the global assessment report on biodiversity and ecosystem services (summary for policy makers). IPBES Plenary at its seventh session (IPBES 7, Paris, 2019)*, 105 and Lorna Inniss et al., *The First Global Integrated Marine Assessment—World Ocean Assessment I, available at* https://www.un.org/regularprocess/content/first-world-ocean-assessment, United Nations (2016).

95 Bacchi, *Analysing policy: what's the problem represented to be?*.

the impossible.[96] Where a policy or regulation is more ambiguous, thus leaving open more choices or providing a wide margin of appreciation to those instigating the measures, decisions, revising regulations, or operationalizing ideas, the implementation becomes more complex.[97] Røvik differentiates between implementation and translation theories, where implementation theory reflects the dominant hierarchical top-down doctrine in which ideas to be implemented are understood as fixed, physical phenomena that are implemented as technical rational installments and those implementing are viewed as passive receivers.[98]

Translation theory, as per Røvik, provides an "alternative doctrine for implementation."[99] Translation theory involves a more or less deliberate transformation of practices and/or ideas that happens when various actors try to transfer and implement them.[100] Thus, from the perspective of translation theory, the policy or regulation is transformed or changed in the course of the translation or implementation. Further, as per Røvik, the translation is highly dependent on the actors responsible for the translation, how well they know the origin of the ideas, and the contexts (arenas) within which these ideas are translated.[101] Often, more than one translator is involved, meaning that more translations could be combined into chains of translations.[102] Translation theory has had little focus in legal scholarship as a perspective of operationalizing law, yet it could be similarly applicable to legal norms or concepts that leave space for discretion of authority or interpretations, such as the ecosystem approach.[103]

---

96 These four criteria are some of those suggested by Brunnée and Toope to identify interactional law, as per Jutta Brunnée and Stephen J. Toope, *Legitimacy and Legality in International Law: An Interactional Account*, Cambridge Studies in International and Comparative Law, (Cambridge: Cambridge University Press, 2010), 6.

97 Gunnar Sander, "Implementation of Ecosystem-Based Ocean Management." (PhD diss., UiT The Arctic University of Norway, 2018), 33.

98 Kjell Arne Røvik, "Translasjon—en alternativ doktrine for implementering," in *Reformideer i norsk skole: Spredning, oversettelse og implementering*, ed. Kjell Arne Røvik, Tor Vidar Eilertsen, and Eli Moksnes Furu (Oslo: Cappelen Damm akademisk, 2014): 403, 411. In addition to the implementation theory (and the translation theory) is the professional theory, a 'bottom-up' doctrine, focusing on the implementers as dominant to implementation rather than the politicians imposing ideas. This research does not look further into the professional theory. Røvik explains this theory on p. 112.

99 Røvik, "Translasjon—en alternativ doktrine for implementering."

100 Ibid, 411.

101 Ibid, 411.

102 Ibid.

103 Lena Schøning, "A methodology to evaluate the ecosystem approach in laws and policies," Iva Parlov and Endalew Lijalem Enyew eds. *NCLOS blog, Norwegian Centre for the Law of the Sea*, 2022. Maria Hammer, "Lost in Translation—Following the Ecosystem Approach from Malawi to the Barents Sea," Arctic Review on Law and Politics, 14 (2023), 46–69.

As implementation or translation takes place in a governance institution or organization, the context of that structure, such as the culture and capacity, as well as parallel processes and other influences, may facilitate or hinder the implementation or translation.[104]

Monitoring means to observe and check the progress or quality of something over a period of time or to keep something under systematic review. The 'something' or object of monitoring could refer to monitoring the implementation or translation (such as the progress or quality), monitoring the output of these actions (e.g., setting up marine protected areas), or, at least ideally, monitoring the outcome or achievement (such as any measurable change in the marine environment). In ocean governance, depending on the purpose of each policy or regulation, the outcome or achievements are sometimes specific, such as that of reducing certain emissions, reducing pressures on a local marine ecosystem by setting up marine protected areas, or facilitating activities such as emerging offshore renewable energy production or seabed mining. Other policies and regulations could have more ambiguous purposes, such as striving for good status of marine ecosystems while facilitating an increase in maritime activities. As any marine ecosystem is under multiple influences, locally, regionally, and globally, it will often be challenging, if not impossible, to monitor the outcome if the purpose is not specific. Often, one would be left with identifying reference points representing what the policy or decision intends to achieve (such as environmental indicators) or representing any major driver to an achievement that one depends on (such as necessary technological development whether for carbon sequestration and storage, to reduce environmental effects of shipping, or the degree and predictions of a green shift). The status of marine ecosystems is often an important reference point in ocean governance. Combined with historical status reports, it may indicate whether the overall trend is improving or not, thus providing one input to whether current measures to reduce negative influences on marine ecosystems are satisfactory or should be intensified.[105]

The final phase is the evaluation and adaptation phase. The results of the monitoring phase form one input to the subsequent evaluation and

---

104 One example of a study using a different translation theory to marine spatial planning is Daniela Pedroza Páez et al., "Understanding translation: Co-production of knowledge in marine spatial planning," *Ocean & Coastal Management* 190 (2020): 105163.

105 The global trend is negative as per Inniss et al., *The First Global Integrated Marine Assessment—World Ocean Assessment I, available at* https://www.un.org/regularprocess/content/first-world-ocean-assessment; Díaz et al., *IPBES 2019: Summary for policymakers of the global assessment report on biodiversity and ecosystem services (summary for policy makers). IPBES Plenary at its seventh session (IPBES 7, Paris, 2019).*

adaptation phase. Evaluation could be envisioned as evaluation of implementation or translation, such as individual decisions (such as industrial permits, emission permits, or establishment of marine protected areas) or their output; evaluation of a policy or regulation in light of new knowledge, such as updates on the status of marine ecosystems or influences on them; evaluation in light of new ideas or connections, such as blue growth or planetary ecosystem processes; evaluation of one or more governance instruments; or evaluation of an institution or a societal need or objective or reference point (such as ecological status or carbon dioxide (CO_2) levels), independent of individual governance instruments. Any responses (or adaptation) desired in respect of such evaluation depend on the set of knowledge inputs and influences, similar to that gathered in the knowledge gathering and analysis phase, which section 3 will unpack.

Engaging stakeholders to achieve broad participation in management processes is an ideal that section 3.3 will discuss. In the context of process phases, it can be noted that participation can be envisioned in different process phases. If influence by participation is a preference, involving stakeholders in the knowledge gathering and analysis phase, in which the remaining process is framed, is arguably the phase that has most bearing and influence on the remaining process. Another important phase, aside the policy and decision-making phase, is the implementation phase, which determines whether the process remains a paper exercise or leads to desired change.

Although this presentation of governance structures and governance processes has drawn on examples from ocean governance, it remains to emphasize that, as is the case with both the aforementioned structural risks of fragmentation and the management process phases, they are no different whether the matter is terrestrial or marine or whether the matter concerns facilitating defense interests or managing taxation or education. Further, the processes and structural risks are no different whether the governance unit is an organization, a state, a public entity, or a private company.[106] Certainly, these inherent structural risks and processes of generic governance are also relevant to ocean governance.

The question emerges as to whether these structural risks or management processes and process phases have particular relevance for ocean governance? Scholarship in ocean governance focusing on processes is vast[107] (noting,

106 Quist and Hellström, "Process Management as a Contagious Idea: A Contribution to Røvik's Virus-Inspired Theory," 902.

107 For example, Ehler, Zaucha, and Gee, "Maritime/Marine Spatial Planning at the Interface of Research and Practice," 1; Gilek, Saunders, and Stalmokaitė, "The Ecosystem Approach

however, that scholars approach, specify, or delimit governance and management processes differently).[108] For example, one paper on marine spatial planning explains that:

> an ecosystem approach which incorporates monitoring and evaluation as well as adaptation as part of its framework can promote understanding, provide data to scientists, inform policy making and help to make effective management decisions.[109]

Thus, the citation refers to phases of the aforementioned generic management process to substantiate the ecosystem approach. While explanatory research and management initiatives on ocean governance may focus on a selection of structural risks and process phases, normative perspectives should arguably emphasize why specific structural risks or a process phase is emphasized at the expense of others, whether it poses a specific problem in or solution to ocean governance, or what the limits of such an argument are. The question of any particular relevance to ocean governance of these structural and process aspects generic to governance arguably remains open.

2.3 *Ideals and Standards of Governance*

This section elaborates how governance is inspired by ideals and standards. Unlike end goals or objectives (such as, a prosperous society or a protected environment), as per the approach, ideals and standards reflect general values, for

---

and Sustainable Development in Baltic Sea Marine Spatial Planning: The Social Pillar, a 'Slow Train Coming'," 162; Winther et al., "Integrated ocean management for a sustainable ocean economy;" Varjopuro, "Evaluation of Marine Spatial Planning: Valuing the Process, Knowing the Impacts"; Gunnar Sander, "Against all odds? Implementing a policy for ecosystem-based management of the Barents Sea," *Ocean & Coastal Management* 157 (2018): 111–23; Fred P. Saunders, Michael Gilek, and Ralph Tafon, "Adding People to the Sea: Conceptualizing Social Sustainability in Maritime Spatial Planning," in *Maritime Spatial Planning: Past, present, future*, ed. Jacek Zaucha and Kira Gee (Cham: Palgrave Macmillan, 2019), 190–193; Christina Kelly et al., "Investigating options on how to address cumulative impacts in marine spatial planning," *Ocean & Coastal Management* 102 (2014): 139–48. Confirming that studies focusing on the 'realities' of ocean management are rare—see Jones, Lieberknecht, and Qiu, "Marine spatial planning in reality: Introduction to case studies and discussion of findings," 263.

108 These differences may reflect different ontological positions. For example, a focus on the production and consumption *process* of documents rather than their content, style, or structure could imply, for example, a phenomenologist position unlike a realist position. Justesen and Mik-Meyer, *Qualitative research methods in organisation studies*, 121–122.

109 Kelly et al., "Investigating options on how to address cumulative impacts in marine spatial planning," 144.

example, that ocean governance should be participatory, integrated, ecosystem based (or based on an ecosystem approach), science based, and based on the rule of law. These examples of ideals and standards are typical to ocean governance, in the sense that ocean governance policy initiatives and scholarship frequently refer to these ideals and standards of governance.[110] These ideals and standards combine components of governance, science, and law. Some of them are even posed as important responses to the problems of the ocean. For example, in the foreword to the Second World Ocean Assessment, UN Secretary-General António Guterres states that the assessment "advises that, to ensure, sustainability, we must work together to improve integrated ocean management."[111]

These ideals and standards involve, among other things, ways of describing governance structures and processes. They emphasize certain ways of organizing structures or processes. For governance to be participatory, it may involve a participatory process that is open to the public and transparent, or a participatory structure may be under the leadership of a parliament or democratically elected leaders. For governance to be integrated, it could combine governance processes, or it could be organized in a top-down structure. The example illustrates how some ways of describing governance structures and processes come with negative or positive connotations, such as top-down governance rather than integrated governance. Nonetheless, top-down instruction can be justified as a way of ensuring integration (or coherence), such as governance organized under one leader (or a group of leaders) that sets common standards for, for example, how governance should be conducted. The example further illustrates how some ideals and standards are ideas of the time (typically participation), often contrasting previous ones.[112] To complement previous perceptions

---

110 In searches of three journals covering ocean governance issues (*Marine Policy*, *ICES Journal of Marine Science*, and *Ocean Development & International Law*), the journals' search tools returned, respectively, 921, 37, and 589 hits for 'participatory process'; 352, 138, and 508 hits for 'science-based'; 3109, 3147, and 244 hits for 'ecosystem approach'; 2370, 3606, and 431 hits for 'integrate'; and 2325, 7, and 796 hits for 'rule of law.' The searches were conducted on January 9 and February 2 and 3, 2023. Readers may note that while these searches indicate a pattern, these keywords are not only used in the context or meaning that this study attaches to them.

111 For example, as per the foreword of the Ruwa et al., *The Second World Ocean Assessment—World Ocean Assessment II, available at* https://www.un.org/regularprocess/woa2launch, by UN Secretary-General António Guterres, "The Assessment advises that, to ensure sustainability, we must work together to improve integrated ocean management."

112 For example, "Traditional silo-structured management, focusing on a single species or sector, is widely seen as insufficient," Rachel D. Long and et al., "Key Principles of

of top-down or silo-structured management, new perspectives of bottom-up and integrated governance have emerged.[113]

Some ideals and standards could often be highlighted by a certain group taking a special interest in them, such as legal scholars highlighting the need for the rule of law or marine scientists highlighting the need for science-based marine management. While, certainly, there are multiple good reasons for governance based on the rule of law and science, an additional reason relevant for these groups is that it emphasizes the relevance of their work.

Unquestionably, the ideals and standards of governance bring enriching perspectives by highlighting certain values or arguments. They are often framed as universally relevant. However, arguably, relevant counterarguments exist to any of them. Participation in governance processes is time-consuming and risks that strong interest groups emphasize their own interests at the expense of collective interests. Integration for some purpose (such as the overlap in time and space of sectoral activities) means less integration from another perspective (such as sectoral integration). Science-based management could risk undermining relevant interests which are not made evident by scientific means (as section 3.3 will explain in more detail). Coherence for some purpose means less coherence from another perspective (as section 2.3 has explained), and, moreover, "a set of coherent but wrong national policies will not achieve fisheries sustainability,"[114] reflecting the limits of the perspective of coherence. Predictability (one aspect of the rule of law as section 4.3 will explain) may cement existing privileges at the expense of humans or ecosystems with fewer privileges.

Despite the fact that these ideals and standards often are presented as universal or a necessity, the relevance of such ideals and standards to any governance issue or research question arguably demands justification, such as why a particular ideal or standard is emphasized at the expense of others, what the

---

Marine Ecosystem-Based Management," *Marine Policy* 57 (2015): 53–60, 53; "Modern good governance shifts decision-making toward (…) ecosystem-oriented integrated management", Anthony Charles, "People, Oceans and Scale: Governance, Livelihoods and Climate Change Adaptation in Marine Social–Ecological Systems," Current Opinion in Environmental Sustainability 4, no. 3 (2012): 351–57, 352; and "it is increasingly evident that modern governance processes require more sophisticated techniques than administrative solutions and top-down directives", Charles Ehler, Jacek Zaucha, and Kira Gee, "Maritime/Marine Spatial Planning at the Interface of Research and Practice," in Maritime Spatial Planning: Past, Present, Future, ed. Jacek Zaucha and Kira Gee (Cham, UK: Palgrave Macmillan, 2019), 1–21, 10.

113 Examples in footnote 112.

114 Young, "Regime Interaction in Creating, Implementing and Enforcing International Law," 93.

counterarguments are, why a particular ideal or standard is relevant to a specific research question or governance issue, and the limits of the justification of the ideal or standard. Since these ideals and standards reflects values, this study finds that the term 'ideals and standards' better reflect a value-laden theoretical conception in contrast to referring to them as concepts.

Three ideals and standards will be dealt with in more detail going forward. The ideal or standard of science-based decision-making and precaution will be discussed in the science section (3.3), rule of law in the law section (4.3), and some ideals and standards that traverses the science–policy interface (cross-sectoral, integrated, and holistic approaches and the ecosystem-based approach) in section 5.1.[115]

The examples of ideals and standards used in this section, which are frequently referred to in ocean governance policy initiatives and literature, are not just relevant to ocean governance. Participation, integration, science, and the rule of law are ideals relevant to any kind of governance. The ecosystem approach is relevant to governance that interferes with ecosystems (terrestrial and ocean governance). Thus, while these ideals and standards are frequently referred to in ocean governance, they are further relevant to other kinds of governance, and in this sense generic.

2.4 *Substance of Governance Instruments (Policies and Regulations)*

This section interrogates what ocean governance is when structures and processes as per section 2.2 and ideals and standards as per section 2.3 are kept outside. This section discusses ocean governance rather than generic governance. This reflects the assumption that the governance structures and processes of section 2.2 are generic to governance and the ideals and standards of section 2.3 are applicable beyond ocean governance. Accordingly, one main component that separates ocean governance from other types of governance is (or at least could be) the substance.

Now imagine looking beyond an optimal governance process in an optimal governance structure complying with the highest of ideals and standards—what is the substance, or what are the merits, of ocean governance? How is it possible to identify, design, or evaluate it? Multiple ways of approaching substantive issues of governance could be envisioned, such as approaching the societal objectives, end goals, or priorities it pursues (addressing ocean

115 Noting that, for example, the science-based decision-making standard and the precautionary principle could belong both in the science section, as they emphasize the role of science, and in the section with those ideals and standards who traverse the science-policy interface.

warming, for example by mitigating climate change) and the strategies and instruments (policies and regulation to that end) it chooses, the institutional implementation or translation of those strategies (how reduction of greenhouse gas (GHG) emissions is pursued for instance by an aquacultural directorate), or the output (GHG emission reduction) or outcome (represented by CO_2 levels in the atmosphere or related ocean temperatures) of governance. Now one may even ask whether mitigating climate change is a matter of ocean governance. Although climate change is a useful example of various substantive approaches to governance, it ultimately depends on how one defines ocean governance, which will be further explained. Empirical case studies could also be a way to approach substantive issues of governance, unless they focus on structures and processes, as Jones et al. finds that studies focusing on the 'realities' of ocean governance are rarer.[116]

This section focuses on the fundamental substantive design of governance instruments, including policies (white papers, plans, strategies, or programs) and regulation such as statutory acts or regional or international treaties. As per Kooiman:

> The systemic nature of state or public governance is mainly due to the use of two major instruments, laws and policies. For almost any subject, on almost every level of public involvement in societal affairs, laws, policies or combinations of the two, are standard governance practices.[117]

Thus, Kooiman regards policies and regulations as standard governance practices. Further, the Science Advice for Policy by European Academies (SAPEA) group of experts that advise the European Commission (SAPEA) classifies design and evaluating strategies as one key function of science for policymaking.[118] It should, however, be noted that the extent to which regulations and policies are able to facilitate the desired outcome depends on many factors beyond their design or content, including power, capacity, institutional culture and purpose, and conflicting regulations and policies. The undertaken approach to substance could be located in the management process phase of policy- and decision-making with regard to objectives and priorities, and tools and strategies.

---

116 Jones, Lieberknecht, and Qiu, "Marine spatial planning in reality: Introduction to case studies and discussion of findings."

117 Kooiman, *Governing as Governance*, 123.

118 Science Advice for Policy by European Academies, *Making Sense of Science Under Conditions of Complexity and Uncertainty* (Berlin: SAPEA, 2019), 59, classifies design and evaluating strategies as one key function of science for policymaking.

Plural approaches to the fundamental substantive design of governance instruments relevant to ocean governance could be envisioned. The design of these instruments may be approached, for example, by mapping their geographically delimited area of application (where); which existing or emerging activities interfering with marine ecosystems are facilitated or restricted or how to protect and preserve marine ecosystems, areas, or components thereof and what to regulate in that respect (what and how); the relevant actors and demands of those actors (who); or the purpose of the governance instrument, such as contributing to one or more societal objectives or a more specific desirable outcome (why). Each of these approaches will be explained in brief as follows, including some inherent premises or priorities vested in them. The approaches may also reflect different understandings of what ocean governance captures, whether the management of marine spaces, maritime activities, activities interfering with marine ecosystems, coastal communities and other ocean actors, or protection (and sustainable use) of marine ecosystems.

The first approach is a spatial one that targets a geographically limited area such as an ocean area or a coastal area covering land and sea areas. However, areas are not governed as such but rather humans whose activities and behavior result in certain profits or benefits yet impact or interfere with the ecosystems of these areas. Nonetheless, the partition underlying governance instruments often involves dividing areas into geographically delimited units. The delimitation could be determined based on administrative reasons, such as parallel to some administrative border, an example of which is the Svalbard Environmental Protection Act of Norway, which applies to the territory and territorial waters of Svalbard. Or the delimitation could be determined by the logic of a socially defined 'natural' system,[119] such as the integrated ocean management plan for the Beaufort Sea of Canada.[120]

The second approach targets the 'what and how' in ocean governance, which naturally depend on what one perceives as ocean governance and the purpose of addressing it. Subject to the focus of this section on policies and regulations, some may perceive ocean governance as those policies and regulations that label themselves marine policies, maritime regulation, ocean management policies, and beyond. Others may perceive ocean governance as the management of maritime activities, which roughly speaking are those activities that depend on ocean space or marine resources. Yet others may perceive ocean governance as

119 David Langlet, "Scale, space and delimitation in marine legal governance—Perspectives from the Baltic Sea," *Marine Policy* 98 (2018): 278–85, 279.

120 Source: https://www.beaufortseapartnership.ca/integrated-ocean-management/integrated-oceans-management-plan/ (last accessed 25 April 2023).

the management of marine ecosystems. Since one does not govern ecosystems, but the humans embedded in them, at least in theory, one could imagine the governance of marine ecosystems to equal the governance of those activities that interfere with marine ecosystems. Yet, as most (maritime or land-based) activities do interfere with marine ecosystems (such as inducing some pollution, waste, or GHG emissions), a selection or delimitation of these activities is often required. The selection would depend on the purpose, and could reflect, for example, those with most (or least) negative effects, those that contribute to the main threats (such as overfishing), those that induce local pressures, or those that comply with a defined frame for, or limit of, (sustainable) use.

The third substantive approach targets the relevant actors (who) and demands placed on those actors. Actors relevant to ocean governance span coastal communities, to 'ocean managers'—or other definitions of public administrators, regulators, or leaders, and further to those economic actors of maritime businesses that operate in an ocean area. A coastal community may consist of many voices and may convey its own economic interests, the interests of its local ecosystems or local area, or global stewardship. The public administrators, regulators, or leaders relevant to ocean governance may be those that have a formal mandate over marine ecosystems or humans and activities interfering with these ecosystems. Institutionally, the 'ocean managers' may be under the specific interests of, for example, a ministry (e.g., trade and industry or of the environment) or further subunit. For example, the (offshore) Norwegian Petroleum Directorate's "main goal is to contribute to the greatest possible value for society from the oil and gas industry through effective and responsible resource management."[121] The extent to which institutional goals impact policy-making and decision-making by leaders and caseworkers depends on, among other factors, the context of that institution, including culture and capacity. The third group of actors are the economic actors, who predominantly would be private companies. Economic objectives and profitability are the important concerns of private companies.[122] Although

---

121 Source: https://www.npd.no/om-oss/ (last accessed 25 April 2023), author's translation from Norwegian.

122 Beate Sjåfjell, "Towards a Sustainable Development: Internalising Externalities in Norwegian Company Law," *International and Comparative Corporate Law Journal* 6, no. 1 (2010): 103–136. For example, relevant to private companies, Sjåfjell explains: "The vast impact that the operations of companies today, on an aggregated level, have on the global economy, on society in general and on the biosphere and the atmosphere, means that a critical analysis of the purpose of companies and regulatory framework within which they operate is crucial to a deeper understanding of the correlation between society and sustainable development," 107.

some companies may prioritize a broader set of objectives,[123] the social norms of shareholder primacy and profitability dominance arguably may shape the decisions and priorities made by these actors.[124] The demands to different ocean actors could therefore reflect interests they represent, a given mandate, legal requirements, or social norms.

The fourth substantive approach targets the purpose or societal objective of a governance instrument. Some objectives frequently referred to by ocean governance instruments are the sustainable use of a marine resource or a marine area;[125] the conservation, protection or preservation of marine ecosystems, areas, or ecosystem components such as species;[126] economic value creation or strengthening and development of maritime industries;[127] and employment and settlement or development of coastal communities.[128] The objectives could often be combined, which may mean they are competing or conflicting. However, in ocean governance, the different objectives may be competing or conflicting, such as in facilitating emerging ocean industries or protecting ocean areas against increased use and activities (noting how increased use of marine space is one of the main threats to the global marine environment as per two recent global assessments).[129] As Bacchi and Goodwin have shown, societal objectives or problems are created through their representation—policies (and scholarly literature) produce certain 'problems,'[130] which represent some assumptions and values and exclude others. Alternative conceptions of objectives of ocean governance could revolve around those that are less represented by the current discourses: ocean or nature, women,

123 Beate Sjåfjell, "Redefining Agency Theory to Internalize Environmental Product Externalities," in *Preventing Environmental Damage from Products: An Analysis of the Policy and Regulatory Framework in Europe*, ed. Carl Dalhammar, Eléonore Maitre-Ekern, and Hans Christian Bugge (Cambridge: Cambridge University Press, 2018): 101.

124 Sjåfjell, "Redefining Agency Theory to Internalize Environmental Product Externalities."

125 For example, art 2 High Seas Biodiversity Treaty.

126 For example, the preamble of UNCLOS.

127 For example, the EU Blue Growth Strategy aimed to support sustainable growth in the marine and maritime sectors, source: https://blue-action.eu/policy-feed/blue-growth (last accessed 6 November 2023).

128 For example, Food and Agriculture Organization of the United Nations, "FAO Voluntary Guidelines for Securing Sustainable Small-Scale Fisheries in the Context of Food Security and Poverty Eradication," (2015).

129 Patricio Bernal et al., "Chapter 54. Overall Assessment of Human Impacts on the Oceans," in *The First Global Integrated Marine Assessment—World Ocean Assessment I*, ed. Lorna Inniss et al. (United Nations General Assembly, 2016); Díaz et al., *IPBES 2019: Summary for policymakers of the global assessment report on biodiversity and ecosystem services (summary for policy makers). IPBES Plenary at its seventh session (IPBES 7, Paris, 2019)*.

130 Bacchi and Goodwin, "Making and Unmaking 'problems'."

local communities, future generations, species beyond the human species. Alternative objectives reflecting different assumptions and values could be nature-centered coexistence;[131] sustainable use by all marine species; protection against human activities; development of industries of local coastal communities; development of gender equal blue businesses;[132] blue justice;[133] blue communities;[134] preservation for future generations; or multispecies justice.[135]

Moreover, the stated objectives of any governance instrument do not exist in a vacuum. Similar or different competing or conflicting objectives could be evident in the governance instrument. For example, protection of the marine environment could be part of an objective of a statutory act on sustainable seabed mining, yet implicit choices to the detriment of the environment are already made if such act facilitates exploitation of seabed minerals. A combination of objectives stated in governance instruments could be appropriate for some purposes, such as framing of the governance instrument. The stated objectives of a governance instrument could also be impacted by the mandate that reflects the partition underlying a governance instrument and governance units. For example, a policy or act on protection of the marine environment that does not include a mandate over behavior or activities that induce pressure on it, would have a limited potential of operationalization of the stated objective. The institutional unit responsible for the implementation or translation of the governance instrument could also impact on the stated objectives of a governance instrument by translating or interpreting them in specific ways. In the example of the statutory act on sustainable seabed mining, locating it administratively under a ministry of trade and industries or a ministry of environment could impact on how the objectives are interpreted and weighed against other objectives. Furthermore, the stated objective could be competing or conflicting with the purpose vested in the actors licensed to act under it.

131 Margherita Paola Poto, *Enviromental law and governance: The helicoidal pathway of participation; A study of a nature-based model inspired by the Arctic, the Ocean, and Indigenous Views* (Torino: Giappichelli, 2022).

132 On gender and businesses, see Roseanne Russell, "Companies and Unconscious Bias: A Case Study on the Need for Interdisciplinary Scholarship," in *Interdisciplinary Research for Sustainable Business: Perspectives of Women Business Scholars*, ed. Beate Sjåfjell, Roseanne Russell, and Maja Van der Velden (Cham: Springer International Publishing, 2023): 169.

133 Nathan James Bennett et al., "Blue growth and blue justice: Ten risks and solutions for the ocean economy," *Marine policy* 125 (2021): 104387.

134 Lisa M. Campbell et al., "From Blue Economy to Blue Communities: reorienting aquaculture expansion for community wellbeing," *Marine policy* 124 (2021): 104361.

135 Danielle Celermajer et al., "Multispecies justice: theories, challenges, and a research agenda for environmental politics," *Environmental politics* 30, no. 1–2 (2021): 119–40.

Resource use and exploitation by economic actors, such as for seabed mining, entails providing roles to actors guided by corporate objectives.

3 Science from a Governance Perspective

3.1 *Introduction to Science*

The question for this section is how science is relevant to structures and processes; ideals and standards; and the substance of governance instruments. This question demands, initially, an introduction to the term 'science' and the governance–science interface in the context of this study. Investigating science from the governance perspective of this study entails approaching science as an influence on, or input into, governance, thus approaching it as data, findings, input, or knowledge produced, rather than as a discipline or beyond. Some take the term 'science' to embrace only the natural sciences, while others also include humanities and social sciences (similar to the meaning of 'research').[136] In the field of study of ocean governance, 'science' is often coupled with 'marine' to form 'marine science,' referring to the marine parts of the natural sciences.[137] This study will use the term in different meanings as specified, yet focus on marine science and science in an ocean governance context.

Science is sometimes modelled as a hierarchical knowledge relationship in which scientific knowledge, in particular the knowledge of the physical sciences, is elevated above other forms of knowledge.[138] This study does not assume such hierarchy of knowledge. While this study focuses on science and therefore knowledge created, developed, or produced by scientific means in accordance with scientific standards, it recognizes that there are different ways of knowing, including local, traditional, and indigenous ways, which are out-of-scope of this study.

Science is created, developed, or produced for different purposes. Science could be described as "experimental or theoretical work undertaken primarily to acquire new knowledge of the underlying foundation of phenomena and

136 For example, Boesch, "The role of science in ocean governance", whose "views are offered from the perspective of a natural scientist," 190. Contrastingly, Science Advice for Policy by European Academies, *Making Sense of Science Under Conditions of Complexity and Uncertainty* includes social and natural science in its definition.

137 Examples from the literature using the terms science and marine science interchangeably includes McConney et al., "A First Look at the Science-Policy Interface for Ocean Governance in the Wider Caribbean Region."

138 MacDonald et al., *Science, information, and policy interface for effective coastal and ocean management*, 56.

observable facts" or, more succinctly, as "original investigation to acquire new knowledge."[139] Science could be classified into basic science or applied science, where basic science "centers on knowledge creation within science itself (...) without any particular application or use in view."[140] Despite the fact that basic science has no particular application in view, when it is created, developed, or produced, it could certainly be relevant for governance. For example, knowledge on ocean acidification was developed as basic science.[141] Applied science, in contrast to basic science, is "directed primarily towards a specific practical aim or objective"[142] from the beginning.[143] The practical aim or objective could be a business objective, such as exploring a marine resource for the purpose of producing food or medications, or a governance objective, such as assessing or monitoring the environmental status of a marine area. A key difference between basic research and applied research is the degree of freedom to frame or approach the research. For applied science, the framing of, or approach to, the research would be limited (to various degrees) by the announcement of funds or a mandate (reflecting the governance or other purpose). Basic science, in contrast, leaves more space for scientists to frame and approach the research to be conducted.

Furthermore, science is created, developed, or produced in diverse ways subject to various dimensions. The science creation, development, or production could be organized under the auspices of a permanent institution (whether a university or a research institute or body such as the International Arctic Science Committee)[144] or a temporary project organization. The monetary funding of science could be permanent or ad hoc. The research body could be independent (such as the International Council for the Exploration of the Sea)[145] or embedded in an organization with a purpose going beyond research (such as the scientific working groups of the Arctic Council).[146] These

---

139 Robert J. W. Tijssen, "Discarding the 'basic science/applied science' dichotomy: A knowledge utilization triangle classification system of research journals," *Journal of the American Society for Information Science and Technology* 61, no. 9 (2010): 1842–52.

140 Tijssen, "Discarding the 'basic science/applied science' dichotomy: A knowledge utilization triangle classification system of research journals."

141 Ken Caldeira and Michael E. Wickett, "Anthropogenic carbon and ocean pH," *Nature* 425, no. 6956 (2003): 365–65.

142 Tijssen, "Discarding the 'basic science/applied science' dichotomy: A knowledge utilization triangle classification system of research journals."

143 MacDonald et al., *Science, information, and policy interface for effective coastal and ocean management*, 51, describe some other approaches.

144 Source: https://iasc.info/about (last accessed 25 April 2023).

145 Source: https://www.ices.dk/about-ICES/Pages/default.aspx (last accessed 25 April 2023).

146 Source: https://arctic-council.org/about/working-groups/ (last accessed 25 April 2023).

and other institutional, organizational, and financial dimensions of science creation, development, or production impact the creation, development, and production of science and, likely, also the output.

The relationship between science and governance is often referred to as the science–policy interface or science–policy interaction. As per the terminology of this study, 'policy' refers to one type of governance instrument, rather than capturing all of governance. Therefore, the governance–science term will mainly be used; however, where science–policy interface is a more precise description, such as in referring to the scholarship on the science–policy interface,[147] it will be referred to as such. This study investigates a one-way approach to this interface, science as input to governance (unlike approaching it as two-way interaction).

Yet even the one-way governance–science relationship may be perceived or modeled in different ways.[148] These models may be more or less implicit and inherent in different approaches, for example based on ontological positions. At one end of the continuum, one model merits science as "offering disinterested, objective advice, while it falls to political actors to make judgements of value."[149] This traditional and, as per Jasanoff,[150] realism (or positivist) notion of scientific knowledge "implies that truths about the natural world arise in an autonomous domain of science, cleanly separated from social influence and the uses of political power."[151] At the other end of the continuum, one could model the science–governance relationship by meriting the role of scientists to "give advice but their input (...) is used selectively and/or strategically to legitimise political choices or depoliticize contentious issues," such as "waiting for the facts" to defer a difficult decision.[152]

---

147 Which was introduced in section 1.1.

148 As per Hoppe, "Scientific advice and public policy: expert advisers' and policymakers' discourses on boundary work:" "Much has been written about the role(s) of scientific expertise in the political arena and public policy. Leaving behind the user-focused, one-directional knowledge utilization model in policy studies, and the co-producer-oriented seamless web model of science/politics interaction in STS studies, contemporary conceptions focus on boundary arrangements and work." Further examples of models, see Pielke, *The honest broker: making sense of science in policy and politics*, 14–18; Rudd, "Scientists' framing of the ocean science–policy interface;" Carol H. Weiss, "The Many Meanings of Research Utilization," *Public administration review* 39, no. 5 (1979): 426–31.

149 Science Advice for Policy by European Academies, *Making Sense of Science Under Conditions of Complexity and Uncertainty*, 54.

150 Jasanoff, *The fifth branch: Science advisers as policymakers*; Jasanoff, *States of Knowledge: The Co-Production of Science and the Social Order*.

151 Boesch, "The role of science in ocean governance," 195.

152 Science Advice for Policy by European Academies, *Making Sense of Science Under Conditions of Complexity and Uncertainty*, 54.

Both models should arguably be critically questioned. While some may consider natural scientific input as truth[153] or 'facts,' such as rising sea levels or warming oceans, presenting scientific findings on such issues will always involve elements of framing, including selection and focus.[154] Such framing includes a chosen research question or verifying a selected hypothesis on the rising of sea levels rather than the variability of sea levels, presentations of relevance and impact (how widespread is ocean warming globally, who are or will be affected and how), and perhaps future predictions, aggregation with other studies, policy options, or recommendations. While these elements would often increase the usefulness of a scientific study from a governance perspective, they are subject to the skills, assumptions, interpretations, intentions, and values of the informing scientists and to the standards of the scientific community. At the governance or policy end of the relationship, the to-be-informed politicians, bureaucrats, or stakeholders similarly have skills, assumptions, interpretations, intentions, and values related to the natural environment, scientific knowledge, and the need to be informed, all of which will influence how they understand and consider the science presented. This study aims to avoid the pitfalls of these models by keeping in mind how science is filtered at both the scientists' and the to-be-informed persons' ends.

To contextualize the filters of scientists and ocean actors, first a note on the practical forms of the governance–science relationship. The governance–science relationship could be envisioned taking different practical forms. One is the form of open and active discussion, such as in a workshop of politicians and bureaucrats, and stakeholders and scientists, such as on alternative ways of problem framing how to address the eutrophication of the Baltic Sea. Another is the form of issuing a report in response to an inquiry (such as on the vulnerability of a certain marine area) that rests on assumptions (asking for evidence of vulnerability rather than evidence of robustness) and demands a certain focus (not asking for the state of the larger environment with which it is intertwined). Other more passive forms of 'interaction' include politicians, bureaucrats, or stakeholders attending a conference where scientists present assessment reports, or scientists publishing a chronicle based on research findings following

153 One may keep in mind how the history of science may indicate how "truth" is historically specific rather than objective and timeless. Bertrum H. MacDonald et al., *Science, Information, and Policy Interface for Effective Coastal and Ocean Management* (Milton, UK: Taylor & Francis Group, 2016), 50.

154 "It is essential to acknowledge (…) that human knowledge is always incomplete and selective, and thus contingent upon uncertain assumptions, assertions and predictions," Science Advice for Policy by European Academies, *Making Sense of Science Under Conditions of Complexity and Uncertainty*, 30.

a scientific expedition that is read by a head of state. Yet another form is scientists being appointed as part of a committee to suggest and prepare a policy or regulation on marine protected areas or to facilitate seabed mining. Notably, many of these interfaces or interactions will only reach some of the politicians that are decision makers or some of the bureaucrats preparing the policy or regulation.

Against the background of these perspectives on science, how it is created, developed, or produced, how it is filtered, and the different forms which the governance–science interface or interaction may take, the question is now how the output of science (data, findings, and conclusions) is relevant to structures and processes, ideals and standards, and the substance of governance instruments.

3.2 *Relevance of Science to Governance Structures and Processes*

3.2.1 Governance Structures

As per section 2.2 governance structures are partitioned into units, entailing a risk of fragmentation, which may be prevented. Partition of governance structures (institutions and organizations) into units may be substantiated by a number of different logics, such as by administrative borders (states, municipalities, regions, or beyond), by topic (climate and pollution), or by activity type (shipping or aquaculture). Scientific and nonscientific input relevant to the logic and substantiation of diverse ways of partitioning governance structures include knowledge of administrative borders, topics, or activity types; problems of existing structures; and improved ways of restructuring or repartitioning. The question emerges whether and how (marine) scientific evidence could or should be used to problematize or justify alternative ways of structuring governance.

Examples exist that scientific evidence such as ecological features or connections are used as arguments for certain structuring of governance, such as in the example of the integrated policy for the Beaufort Sea.[155] While the Beaufort Sea is a naturally connected entity, it is also connected to the surrounding area and the larger and ultimately global natural system. Another example is the European Union (EU) Horizon Europe research program, which includes a component to restore oceans and waters, relying on a report stating[156] that the:

---

155 Source: https://www.beaufortseapartnership.ca/integrated-ocean-management/ (last accessed 25 April 2023).

156 Pascal Lamy et al., *Proposed Mission: Mission Starfish 2030: Restore our Ocean and Waters*, Report of the Mission Board Healthy Oceans, Seas, Coastal and Inland Waters (2020), 46.

> integrity of Europe's entire water system … cannot be managed by dividing it into parts or administratively disconnecting fresh waters from the seas and the ocean.[157]

Similarly, it has been proposed that governance structures should reflect large marine ecosystems.[158] These are arguments of, on one side, ecological connection and, on the other side, disconnection from the greater area or land. The arguments reflect that ecologically speaking some areas or systems are more connected than others. Governance, however, is tightly connected to humans, and in line with the governance definition of this study, one could argue that the objects of governance (as well as political steering or regulation) are humans, human behavior, or human activities, rather than areas or ecosystems. As per this approach, the governing of an area or ecosystem could refer to the governing of humans or the human activities that are situated in that area or that interfere with or induce pressures on these water or marine ecosystems. Therefore, a policy for the Beaufort Sea could be integrated in different ways, managing local activities on or around it or activities that induce pressure on it. Pressures inflicted on the EU's ecologically connected water system (as well as any other marine ecosystems) include climate change, overfishing, and pollution.[159] Although the ecology of the water system reflects that these pressures should all be restricted, arguments for comanaging climate change, overfishing, and pollution would rather be, for example, that they need similar responses or expertise, stem from the same human activities or cause, or need careful adjustments to each other.

Thus, while marine scientific knowledge provides input on significant impacts and their locations, how to partition or structure governance to modify human behavior or activities to that end requires different lines of argumentation related to what those impacts are. Connected ecosystems do not necessarily translate to appropriate governance structuring. For this reason, approaches to the structuring of governance defined by ecosystems or "natural systems"[160] should carefully consider the justification and limits of such approach.

157 Lamy et al., *Proposed Mission: Mission Starfish 2030: Restore our Ocean and Waters*, 44.

158 Lawrence Juda and Timothy Hennessey, "Governance Profiles and the Management of the Uses of Large Marine Ecosystems," *Ocean Development & International Law* 32, no. 1 (2001): 43–69.

159 Díaz et al., *IPBES 2019: Summary for policymakers of the global assessment report on biodiversity and ecosystem services (summary for policy makers). IPBES Plenary at its seventh session (IPBES 7, Paris, 2019)*.

160 Langlet, "Scale, space and delimitation in marine legal governance—Perspectives from the Baltic Sea."

Now that the relevance of science to the governance structures and units have been discussed, the question remains of science's relevance to the risk of fragmentation (which reflects how some topics or perspectives always will be governed across other divisions, topics, or perspectives, or in a 'fragmented' way as per section 2.2) and ways of preventing fragmentation. This very study is an example of how science could be relevant to the risk of fragmentation, by theorizing governance structures.[161] System-based approaches, such as Earth system governance[162] may offer perspectives complementing the partitioning of governance into units. Science could further contribute with studies on ways of preventing fragmentation structurally.

3.2.2 Governance Processes

The next question is the relevance of science to management processes, starting with the knowledge gathering and analysis phase. As per section 2.2, this phase provides for framing and approach, resulting in a collection and selection of knowledge. One fundamental influence of science on this phase (and beyond) involves how it contributes to enlightenment, as in a fundamental understanding of the world.[163] Science is further relevant to orientation, which captures being informed about the state of the art in a specific area and the understanding of a challenge or problematic situation.[164] While enlightenment is, perhaps, more basic and general, and orientation more advanced and specific, these two functions depend on each other and gradually overlap; thus they will be treated in combination going forward. Examples of enlightenment and orientation, relevant to ocean governance, include knowledge of human dependencies on the ocean for protein, energy, and transportation; how humans have

---

161 Other examples of science relevant to the fragmentation of regimes (unlike structures), include, for example, Seline Trevisanut and et al., *Regime Interaction in Ocean Governance*, ed. Seline Trevisanut and et al. (Boston: Boston: Brill, 2020); *Regime Interaction in International Law: Facing Fragmentation*, ed. Margaret A. Young (Cambridge: Cambridge University Press, 2012).

162 For example, Sarah Burch et al., "New directions in earth system governance research," *Earth System Governance* 1 (2019).

163 Science Advice for Policy by European Academies, *Making Sense of Science Under Conditions of Complexity and Uncertainty*.

164 Ibid, at 101, describe the multiple roles of science and scientists in the natural resource and environmental policy process: "Levien argues there are multiple roles on how this can happen. First, scientists can provide background on the basic fundamentals of environmental problems, identifying known processes and those things that are uncertain. Second, scientists can then describe and identify management options for solutions to those problems. Finally, scientists can contribute to environmental problem solving by estimating the environmental and socioeconomic consequences of proposed solutions through time and across population groups."

organized the exchange of goods and services in economic systems; the existence of ecosystems, Earth system processes, and planetary boundaries;[165] the main threats to the global marine environment;[166] and how states have defined and divided entitlements to ocean areas between themselves,[167] which forms the basis for (re)distributing access to resources and marine spaces to private persons, economic entities, and local communities (under national law).

The examples further illustrate how enlightenment and orientation, and therefore science, may influence our values (at least from the perspective of a growth mindset).[168] The science of Earth system processes and planetary boundaries may impact on people's perceptions of whether we value and need to protect the global Earth environment. Scientific research about the existence, history, and conditions of indigenous peoples may influence the desire to prioritize their interests.

Problem framing is another way in which natural and social science contributes to the knowledge gathering and analysis phase. As per SAPEA, a main call to science is "to support policymaking by providing the best available knowledge in understanding a specific problem."[169] Problem framing as a scientific input could be envisioned as redefining or exploring the problem framing of, for example, governance instruments, tools and strategies, or even objectives and priorities. Bardwell, similarly, explains from a cognitive psychology and conflict management perspective how:

> Problem-framing emphasizes focusing on the problem definition. Since how one defines a problem determines one's understanding of and approach to that problem, being able to redefine or reframe a problem and to explore the 'problem space' can help broaden the range of alternatives and solutions examined.

---

165 Johan Rockström, "Planetary Boundaries," *New Perspectives Quarterly* 27, no. 1 (2010): 72–74; Steffen Will et al., "Planetary boundaries: Guiding human development on a changing planet," *Science* 347, no. 6223 (2015): 736–736.

166 Bernal et al., "Chapter 54. Overall Assessment of Human Impacts on the Oceans"; Díaz et al., *IPBES 2019: Summary for policymakers of the global assessment report on biodiversity and ecosystem services (summary for policy makers). IPBES Plenary at its seventh session (IPBES 7, Paris, 2019).*

167 As reflected in UNCLOS.

168 Amy Baldwin et al., *Promoting belonging, growth mindset, and resilience to foster student success* (Columbia, SC: National Resource Center for The First-Year Experience and Students in Transition, University of South Carolina, 2020).

169 Science Advice for Policy by European Academies, *Making Sense of Science Under Conditions of Complexity and Uncertainty*, 12 and 21.

Thus, exploring, mapping, and exposing problem definitions relied on in policies and regulations, framing and reframing the problem space, is one way in which scientific expertise is relevant to the knowledge gathering and analysis phase. SAPEA explains the powerful impact of framing:

> A significant body of work on relations between science (broadly defined) and policy has identified the importance of frames and framing, through which particular problem definitions, knowledge claims and policy options are emphasised (considered to be 'in the frame') whilst others are effectively removed from consideration (Entman, 1993; Vreese, 2005). At any one time, the dominant framing (of an environmental problem, for example) may be so familiar as to be tacit. (…) Just as framing helps to delimit what is 'thinkable', reframing can be a precursor for significant policy change.[170]

Framing the environmental problems of the ocean is a key cross-disciplinary scientific function of science. One example of framing in ocean governance literature is the study of Campbell et al. contrasting normative goals of blue economy with the increased wellbeing of coastal communities, which provides alternative problem framings.[171] In general, framing or problem framing is relevant both to the knowledge gathering and analysis phase and the subsequent policy- and decision-making phase.

Another question is the relevance of scientific input (data, findings, conclusions) to the knowledge gathering and analysis phase. Scientific inputs do not exist in isolation. A number of other inputs and concerns beyond marine scientific input may concurrently compete for attention when gathering knowledge and analyzing ocean matters. These nonscientific and scientific inputs include concerns for employment, social distribution, economic prosperity, and perceptions of possibilities, including that of reelection. An often posed question (which may reflect a realist model of the governance–science interface) is whether and how new scientific input could or should lead to new governance efforts or adaptation of existing governance. For example, should new scientific input on the increasingly negative effects of marine plastics on cetaceans or an increasing need for protein as feed or food lead to a change of policies or regulation? The input may point to numerous ocean and terrestrial policy

170 Science Advice for Policy by European Academies, *Making Sense of Science Under Conditions of Complexity and Uncertainty*, 69–70.

171 Campbell et al., "From Blue Economy to Blue Communities: reorienting aquaculture expansion for community wellbeing."

and regulatory choices, invoking a number of other nonscientific and scientific concerns.

Further, new scientific evidence may be already accounted for in current policies and regulations or may not be enough to change a predefined set of priorities for different concerns. Moreover, new (or existing) scientific evidence may substantiate a number of different political positions. While at least some politicians would claim that current policies and regulations are science informed, arguably, scientific evidence already exists to substantiate radical changes of priorities. For example, status assessments of the global marine environment keep reporting the urgent need to take action to address the main threats to the marine environment, including overfishing, use of marine space, climate change, pollution and waste, and non-native species.[172] While the reduction of these threats is at the focus of governments and beyond, currently no status trends indicate that these threats are sufficiently reduced or mitigated or that the deteriorating trends are shifting. On the contrary, a recent Intergovernmental Panel on Climate Change (IPCC) report on global warming[173] was deemed 'code red for humanity' by the UN Secretary-General, indicating the need for even stronger responses.[174] Thus, the absence of a sufficient governance response to shift the deteriorating trends could be viewed as governance not (sufficiently) informed by science.

Another ocean governance example is the research on marine plastic pollution that points to the need for circular economic models, within regulatory limits, to prevent the increasing amount of plastics accumulating in the ocean.[175] Are current policies and regulations informed of these scientific inputs? If not, are they science informed? How should or could they adapt to facilitate new economic models and economic regulation and which other concerns are invoked by the nature of the different policy responses? These examples illustrate how a claim or an assumption that governance should be based

---

172 Díaz et al., *IPBES 2019: Summary for policymakers of the global assessment report on biodiversity and ecosystem services (summary for policy makers). IPBES Plenary at its seventh session (IPBES 7, Paris, 2019)*; Bernal et al., "Chapter 54. Overall Assessment of Human Impacts on the Oceans."

173 V. Masson-Delmotte et al., *IPCC, 2021: Climate Change 2021: The Physical Science Basis. Contribution of Working Group I to the Sixth Assessment Report of the Intergovernmental Panel on Climate Change*, Cambridge University Press (Cambridge and New York, 2021).

174 UN Secretary-General, "Secretary-General Calls Latest IPCC Climate Report 'Code Red for Humanity', Stressing 'Irrefutable' Evidence of Human Influence," news release, 2021.

175 Sarah J. Morath, *Our plastic problem and how to solve it* (Cambridge: Cambridge University Press, 2022); Marilena Streit-Bianchi, Margarita Cimadevila, and Wolfgang Trettnak, *Mare Plasticum—The Plastic Sea: Combatting Plastic Pollution Through Science and Art*, 1st 2020. ed. (Cham: Springer International Publishing: Imprint: Springer, 2020).

on, or adapt to, new scientific evidence or changes in the marine environment should be nuanced in multiple ways by considering the complicatedness of competing and potentially conflicting scientific and nonscientific inputs relevant to policies and regulation, the multiple policy and regulatory alternatives that scientific evidence may give rise to, the demand for political anchoring or legitimacy of changes or adaptations to policies or regulations, and beyond. Instead of 'science based' or 'evidence based,' some scholars use the term 'evidence informed' to explicitly reflect the fact that multiple concerns are relevant to decisions (such as to adopt or change a governance instrument) in which natural and social science is not the "only one and, on many issues, not even the decisive one."[176] In any event, use of science to inform decisions should also take account of the reliability of the scientific advice, uncertainties, ambiguity, and limits of understanding,[177] as well as interpretations both on the side of the scientists and the politicians and bureaucrats. Arguably, the term 'science-informed' rather than 'science-based' decision-making may better reflect these nuances and how scientific input is one of many concerns.

Another natural and social scientific input to the policy- and decision-making phase, as per SAPEA, is that of designing and evaluating strategies.[178] The goal for this input is to "co-design, evaluate and monitor strategies for reaching a common goal that all actors want to pursue."[179] The scientific input as per this function is not neutral but directed toward predefined normative goals or values. Predefined normative goals or values relevant to ocean governance include, for example, sustainable growth in the marine and maritime sectors,[180] the research on which may indicate how blue growth diverges from, competes with or is hindered by other approaches or law.[181] This advocacy

176 Science Advice for Policy by European Academies, *Making Sense of Science Under Conditions of Complexity and Uncertainty*, 23.

177 Ibid.

178 As per Science Advice for Policy by European Academies, *Making Sense of Science Under Conditions of Complexity and Uncertainty*, another main function is 'integration' or, as per Wolters et al., "What is the best available science? A comparison of marine scientists, managers, and interest groups in the United States," 97: "collaboration and integration among managers and scientists." The author finds that this function is essentially a mix of the other functions (in response to a mix of governance aspects). Therefore, it is not pursued in this research.

179 Science Advice for Policy by European Academies, *Making Sense of Science Under Conditions of Complexity and Uncertainty*, 59.

180 For example, the EU Blue Growth Strategy, available at https://blue-action.eu/policy-feed/blue-growth (last accessed 6 November 2023).

181 Jones, Lieberknecht, and Qiu, "Marine spatial planning in reality: Introduction to case studies and discussion of findings"; Jonas Kyrönviita et al., "Achieving Blue Growth Post-Weser: a Study of Aquaculture Regulation in the Nordic Region," *Journal for European environmental & planning law* 2021, 18, no. 3 (2021): 256–74.

science function entails that science has a specific function relevant to the management process phase that concerns designing and evaluating policy, tools, and strategies with regard to objectives and priorities. This will be discussed in more detail in section 3.4 on the relevance of science to the substance of governance instruments.

The next question is the relevance of science to the implementation and monitoring phase. The social science literature on implementation and translation theory is certainly relevant to an administrative (institutional or organizational) focus on implementation, including how and when implementation or translation is completed. Monitoring may capture the monitoring of implementation (or translation), output, outcome, or any reference points related to the outcome, such as the status of the marine ecosystems. Depending on the purpose or objectives of any policy or regulation, the preferred outcome could either be satisfactory ecological status, prosperous economic activities, a combination of these (such as in 'protection and sustainable use'), or something else. The marine sciences are relevant to the monitoring of one of these potential reference points—ecological status. The results of any monitoring could be used as input to the subsequent evaluation and adaptation phase.

Since the evaluation and adaptation phase is similar to the knowledge gathering and analysis phase, this phase is equally subject to the continuous influence by real-world changes, changing political priorities and trends, changes of perceptions of the world, and changes of ideals, to which the scientific input only provides part of the input. Further, for cyclic or iterative processes, the evaluation of previous problem orientations and framings, efforts, and implementation, will add to the knowledge basis.

To summarize, the relevance of science for governance is in one way broad in providing input to enlightenment, orientation, and values, to problem framing, and as input to the design and evaluation of a range of different policy options. In another way, the relevance of science is limited, in the midst of the streams of real-world changes, changing political priorities and trends, changes of perceptions of the world, and changes of ideals, capturing many concerns of which only some would be scientifically supported, entailing that science is only one of multiple inputs.

3.3 *Relevance of Science in the Ideals and Standards of Governance*

This section asks how the relevance of science to governance is expressed in certain ideals and standards in the literature and governance instruments on ocean governance. Section 3.1 has set out how governance is science informed rather than science based. Further, it has shown how science may support multiple different political positions, including that one could argue that current policies and regulations are not science informed. At an overall level, it is hard to argue against how governance is to some extent science informed. The capacity of governance to be science informed may, if not alone, contribute to governance being perceived as meeting many of the ideals and standards relevant to ocean governance (and governance in general), such as to be good, responsive, and legitimate. Further, science-informed governance could justify that governance processes are participatory, to the extent that scientists participate in them.

One ideal and standard commonly referred to in ocean governance literature,[182] which highlights the relevance of science to governance is the ideal or standard of science-based decision-making. This study has articulated how science may contribute to enlightenment, values, problem orientation, and policy and regulatory design and evaluation, yet provides only one of many concerns informing governance. Further, scientific input may substantiate a number of different policy options or political positions and is subject to interpretations both at the giving-advice end and the receiving-advice end. Therefore, science may inform decision-making implicitly and explicitly, while demanding supplementary knowledge and not pointing to one specific decision.[183] The calls for science-based decision-making should be nuanced in these ways.

I question whether sometimes, in an ocean governance context, the calls for more science-based decision-making are actually calls for emphasizing marine environmental scientific input and, therefore, prioritizing environmental interests more in the decision-making. If this is the case, such calls should preferably be clarified as such, and not framed as calls for 'neutral' scientific inputs, regardless of whether the input furthers economic, social, or environmental interests. On the one hand, persuasive arguments exist to prioritize environmental interests. On the other hand, framing such arguments as 'neutral' (science) points to a distinct set of questions, such as the extent of decision-making that is not science based, is not fact based (or is fake), or is based on misunderstandings, or which interests are furthered by science and which are not. Moreover, while framing arguments to prioritize environmental interests as 'neutral' science may reflect an unintended generalization of certain scientific input as 'science,' the priorities it may mean to argue for are not 'neutral.' For reasons

182 See notes 21 and 40.

183 Similarly, "decision-making is often more complex than 'imagined in the frequently expressed statement that 'science should inform decision-making'. Many factors come into play, including the use of different forms of knowledge, such as anecdotal and traditional information." MacDonald et al., *Science, information, and policy interface for effective coastal and ocean management*, 448.

of transparency and to avoid any scientific bias,[184] calls for science-based decision-making should clarify what is meant by science-based decision-making, whether to prioritize environmental interests, to avoid decision-making based on false assumptions or misunderstandings, to involve only basic science, or something else. Each of these alternative interpretations points to different problems and questions.

Another ideal or standard—frequently referred to in ocean governance, which directly signals the relevance of science to governance—includes the ideal of 'best available science' or similarly formulated standards.[185] It could either be interpreted as a general standard of governance, reflecting how governance should be science informed (or science based).[186] Other times, the ideal is used in particular contexts, for example, the demand to states, as per UNCLOS, to take certain measures for the conservation of living resources of the high seas on the "best scientific evidence available to the States concerned."[187]

Questions remain whether it is possible to identify the relevant or best science in a particular governance situation. This study has highlighted the multiple ways in which science influences governance, and the limited ways in which science provides input to governance. On this premise, the situations where all scientific evidence supports the same option (beyond being best and available), and the extent to which other inputs (such as competing concerns) would be considered irrelevant, would be quite limited. Further, Boesch highlights another concern:

> Rather than the 'best' possible science for policy, we must ask how to achieve the level of certainty needed for real-time political decisions, given that much knowledge about the environment will continue indefinitely to elude the firm grasp of science.[188]

---

184 For example, cognitive bias, such as, "scientific biases associated with academicians' efforts to defend their theories and knowledge assertions," Joseph H. Michalski, "The sociological determinants of scientific bias," *Journal of Moral Education* 51, no. 1 (2022): 47–60, 49.

185 A variety of these formulation in legal instruments was presented by Hilde Woker, at NCLOS conference, 2 Nov 2023.

186 Wolters et al., "What is the best available science? A comparison of marine scientists, managers, and interest groups in the United States."

187 UNCLOS, art 119.

188 Boesch, "The role of science in ocean governance," 195.

Thus, the level of (un)certainty, as highlighted by Boesch, is another reason for questioning the applicability of the best available science standard. The use of this standard should in any event be justified, and its limits specified.

Another standard that concerns uncertainty, which is frequently referred to in ocean governance and beyond and directly signals the relevance of science to governance, is the precautionary approach. The precautionary approach or principle comes in multiple versions and includes several aspects. One aspect, regarded by Sands et al. as the core of the principle,[189] is expressed in Principle 15 of the Rio Declaration, which dates back to 1992. It states that:

> In order to protect the environment, the precautionary approach shall be widely applied by States according to their capabilities. Where there are threats of serious or irreversible damage, lack of full scientific certainty shall not be used as a reason for postponing cost-effective measures to prevent environmental degradation.[190]

This principle is further included in the Convention on Biological Diversity and the UN Framework Convention on Climate Change.[191] The principle states how a lack of full scientific certainty should not preclude certain measures, which invites a brief account on scientific (un)certainty. Scientific uncertainty, as per Hasselman, involves "three broadly recognised types of uncertainty (...): imperfect knowledge, incomplete knowledge and unpredictability."[192] While 'imperfect knowledge' is inadequate or inexact knowledge, which can be reduced through more adequate or exact knowledge, such as science;[193] 'incomplete knowledge,' requires multiple perspectives to construct a full understanding,[194] which as per this study can be reduced by drawing on multiple perspectives

189 Philippe Sands et al., *Principles of international environmental law*, 4th ed. (Cambridge: Cambridge University Press, 2018), 230. For a different approach, Steel discusses the multiple versions or interpretations of the precautionary principle and related concepts in chapter 3 of Daniel Steel, *Philosophy and the Precautionary Principle: Science, Evidence, and Environmental Policy* (Cambridge: Cambridge University Press, 2014).

190 "UNGA/CONF.151/26 (Vol. I) Rio Declaration On Environment And Development," (1992).

191 Convention on Biological Diversity (CBD), adopted June 5, 1992, entered into force 29 December 1993, 1760 UNTS 79; and UNFCCC.

192 Hasselman, "Adaptive management; adaptive co-management; adaptive governance: what's the difference?," which, in contrast to this study, explains these three types in a systems perspective.

193 Similarly, Hasselman, "Adaptive management; adaptive co-management; adaptive governance: what's the difference?"

194 Hasselman, "Adaptive management; adaptive co-management; adaptive governance: what's the difference?"

(scientific and beyond). Unpredictability, resulting from restricted knowledge about the future, is to some extent irreducible.[195] Thus, some level of uncertainty will always be present, both with respect to current knowledge being imperfect and incomplete and as concerns the future. Therefore, different types of uncertainty limit the ways in which science is relevant to governance. The relevance of (uncertain) scientific input may be considered differently depending on how the to-be-informed bureaucrat, politician, parliament, or head of state understands scientific uncertainty.

While some uncertainty is characteristic of science, the precautionary principle invites states to take measures, based on science. As this section has already shown, multiple governance options may emerge in response to, for example, scientific inputs about the marine environment. This is a challenge to the precautionary principle, in that the relevance of science is in one way limited, in being one of multiple inputs, and in other ways broad, in providing input to enlightenment and values (the role of the climate and the usefulness of preserving it), to problem framing (such as how mitigation and adaptation are two different problems), and to the design and evaluation of a range of different policy options (measures taken and measures that could be envisioned to mitigate climate change and adapting in response to its impacts). Nonetheless, the precautionary principle highlights the relevance of science to governance, despite the uncertainty prevailing and the many options it may give rise to.

3.4 *Relevance of Science to the Substance of Governance Instruments*

Governance is under the continuous influence of changing political priorities and trends, real-world changes, changes in perceptions of the world, and changes of ideals. Thus, one could imagine that governance instruments could either respond to, or persist against, streams of, or individual, influences, to which science only provides part of the input yet in diverse ways. This section interrogates how scientific input is relevant to the substance of governance instruments.

The question is first how science is relevant to the spatial approach to governance instruments. As per section 2.4, the partition underlying governance instruments, dividing areas into geographically delimited units, could be determined by arguments of 'natural' systems (beyond administrative and more). Thus, scientific input could be relevant to support where it is more or less 'natural' to draw the lines. For example, in deciding in which areas to

---

195 The 'some extent' intends to capture perspectives such as future studies, scenario thinking, and beyond. The irreducibility is suggested by Hasselman, "Adaptive management; adaptive co-management; adaptive governance: what's the difference?"

plan for expanding blue (marine) economic activities, scientific knowledge on the robustness of ecosystems is relevant (alongside other concerns, such as where most resources are available or accessible, access to infrastructure, and interference with existing activities). Scientific knowledge is equally relevant in determining where to establish marine protected areas, which may be decided based on scientific input regarding which areas are (most) vulnerable (alongside other concerns such as shipping lanes; existing, traditional, and potential new uses of areas; threatened or vulnerable species; capacities and status of the larger marine area to which the protected area belongs; and the degree of protection needed or desired).

Further, science may also inform governance about the importance of scale. Not only are the Earth system processes global in scale,[196] many human pressures have an impact on a global scale.[197] The human impact on any area results from the aggregation of local-, regional-, and global-scale pressures induced on that area over time. Scientific knowledge on the mix of local and global pressures could provide information about the relative relevance of local measures (such as restricting local activities), as opposed to, for example, responses to reduce global pressures (such as national measures to mitigate climate gases).

The second question is how science is relevant to the 'what and how' of governance instruments. Science has a vital role in providing knowledge about (marine) ecosystems in assessment reports. The approach of any scientific reports and assessments will certainly influence what they find and highlight. It may describe threats to an area or different ecosystem components existing in an area. Knowledge about ecosystem components may be considered and used in several ways, whether to support their protection, exploitation, or eradication (if an invasive species). Scientific inputs on the existence of marine resources eligible for human exploitation, such as krill, snow crabs, or hydrothermal vents, may provide for the setting up of policies or regulatory regimes providing for economic exploitation of these resources, while scientific reports of the existence of cold-water reefs may provide for restrictions of use. The policy and regulatory options relevant to such knowledge depend, among other things, on the assessment approach, on values and political positions, on technology, and on accessibility of the component.

---

196 J. Rockstrom et al., "Planetary Boundaries: Exploring the Safe Operating Space for Humanity," *Ecol. Soc.* (2009): 32; Will et al., "Planetary boundaries: Guiding human development on a changing planet."

197 Joseph R. Burger et al., "The Macroecology of Sustainability," *PLoS Biology* 10, no. 6 (2012): e1001345; Lena Schøning, "The Contribution of Integrated Marine Policies to Marine Environmental Protection: The Case of Norway," *International Journal of Marine and Coastal Law* 2 (2021): 5–7.

Further, science has a significant role in providing status reports. Status reports may recommend overall policy choices on how to adopt or revise governance instruments. For example, the IPCC special report of 2019 on the ocean and cryosphere "highlights the urgency of prioritising timely, ambitious, coordinated and enduring action (*very high confidence*)"[198] to mitigate climate change. This scientific input could, for example, translate into reducing climate gas emissions. Advocacy scientific input (section 3.2) in terms of how to reduce such emissions could also be envisioned. In the regulation of industries and granting or withdrawing of permits to operate and emit, whether to upscale or downscale activities, governance instruments may consider the potential impact of individual activities, an entire industry and its life cycle impacts, or the cumulative impacts on a certain area, all of which depend on input from the natural sciences.

Insofar as governance instruments modify human activities or human behavior, which are embedded in and affect the natural environment, the natural science inputs to the design or change of governance instruments are more or less indirect. Sometimes scientific findings in the natural environment can be traced back to an activity and point to more or less specific governance options, such as the tracks from bottom trawling on the seabed pointing to potential modification of bottom trawling (unless regarded, for instance, as tolerable damage or marine cultural landscape). Other times, the activity causing the negative influence is less obvious. For example, scientific findings may indicate that a decline in the population of the key Arctic species of polar cod may be due to ocean warming and oil emissions.[199] The ocean warming stems from the global amount of climate gases, while the oil emissions may not easily be traced to any particular activity or source. Further, any measures to be adopted for the protection of the polar cod population would concern future climate change emissions or oil emissions, which would need to be predicted. Moreover, the current policy risk profile may in any event allow certain negative effects, which again depends on how the oil-emitting activity (whether fisheries, offshore petroleum extraction, or shipping) is valued, and the legal power or authority of the governance actor (such as the limited authority of individual states over shipping or over activities in the high seas). Similarly, the tracks of bottom trawling may point to the activity of trawling yet this raises a number

198 Pörtner et al., *IPCC 2019: Summary for Policymakers. In: IPCC Special Report on the Ocean and Cryosphere in a Changing Climate* (*IPCC special report*), source: https://www.ipcc.ch/srocc/, 35.

199 Morgan Lizabeth Bender et al., "Combined effects of crude oil exposure and warming on eggs and larvae of an arctic forage fish," *Sci Rep* 11, no. 1 (2021): 8410–17.

of questions regarding whether to modify or tolerate the trawling activities, by relocation, stronger gear requirements, avoiding an area, or continuing as before. Thus, any (causal) link between, on the one hand, scientific evidence of human influence on ecosystems (the negative effects of bottom trawling or a decline in the polar cod population) and, on the other hand, human activities or human behavior (many of which lead or may lead to oil pollution and climate gas emissions or drive the demand for fish, oil, or shipping) has multiple ends. Which activity to modify by policy or regulation is not (and will probably never be) entirely clear at the micro decision-making level based on the scientific input.

Perceiving the governance–science interface in a causal way that links scientific input with governance response may have some undesired effects. It may lead to a drive for gathering more knowledge as a means to strengthen the causal link between scientific input and governance response, which will in fact never be clear. Perspectives of aggregation may to some extent remedy the lack of clarity or causal link between scientific input and policy and regulatory options. These may be status trends over time or statuses of multiple studies of larger areas in aggregation. These may point to overall trends rather than individual inputs, resembling climate change trends rather than climate variations. For example, while individual links as per the aforementioned examples are not always clear, the aggregation of multiple scientific assessments nonetheless identifies overfishing and pollution as main pressures or drivers on the global marine ecosystems.[200] Therefore, arguably, what is clear is that overfishing and pollution should be addressed, reduced, and mitigated. Nevertheless, how, where, and by whom, is not given, and other concerns beyond these inputs are also relevant, as section 3.2 has explained.

The fourth question asks for the relevance of science to the demands and design of ocean governance actors. Perceptions of what ocean governance is influence who one sees as relevant actors. Often, multiple actors are envisioned: citizens, communities, private companies, nongovernmental organizations (NGOs), substate entities, states, and international organizations. The scientific knowledge relevant to these groups of actors is somewhat similar and somewhat different. While input relevant to enlightenment, orientation, values, and, to some extent, problem framing may be relevant to all these actors, the combined set of intervention potential of each group of actors differs.

200 Díaz et al., *IPBES 2019: Summary for policymakers of the global assessment report on biodiversity and ecosystem services (summary for policy makers). IPBES Plenary at its seventh session (IPBES 7, Paris, 2019)*; Bernal et al., "Chapter 54. Overall Assessment of Human Impacts on the Oceans."

States have multiple capacities, including that of making and changing policies and regulations, while citizens and NGOs primarily may influence other actors, such as through voting, activism, or as consumers. Private companies may modify their activities and products relevant to different purposes and influence changes through their roles as sector representative, consumer of goods and services, and beyond. Thus, the strategies relevant to different ocean actors diverge, entailing that different advocacy scientific input (to "co-design, evaluate and monitor strategies for reaching a common goal that all actors want to pursue")[201] will be relevant to them. Ocean governance research that identifies solutions and options without diversifying or specifying ocean actors may identify solutions and options that are only available to some of them.

The fifth question concerns the relevance of science to the objectives and purposes of ocean governance. As per section 2.3, some common objectives in ocean governance instruments are the sustainable use of a marine resource or a marine area; the protection or preservation of marine ecosystems, areas, or ecosystem components such as species; economic value creation or the strengthening and development of maritime industries; and employment and settlement in coastal communities. These objectives reflect the current paradigm and, like any objectives, reflect values. Yet, values and objectives are, at least partly, influenced by enlightenment and orientation; therefore, science may also be relevant to the values held by individual scientists, citizens, administrators, and politicians, as well as to the societal objectives that their communities agree on. Objectives reflecting a need to protect or preserve or use the marine ecosystems in an environmentally sustainable way have emerged on the agenda as scientific reporting on the pressures on these environments (as well as the pressures themselves) has increased. For example, in 1972, the UN Conference on the Human Environment was held, drawing international attention to environmental problems.[202] This was the UN's first major conference on environmental problems in general (rather than specific problems),[203] which likely led to stronger focus on environmental problems and therefore, may have influenced some people's perceptions of whether we need to value and protect the environment. Further, more recent research on climate change and planetary boundaries may have changed perceptions of whether we value and need

201 Science Advice for Policy by European Academies, *Making Sense of Science Under Conditions of Complexity and Uncertainty*, 59, section 3.2.

202 Jan H. Jans, "Stop the Integration Principle," *Fordham International Law Journal* 33, no. 5 (2010): 1533–47, 1535. Sands et al., *Principles of international environmental law*, 21–51, provides a more extensive historical account.

203 Resulting in the UNGA/CONF.48/14/Rev.1 Report of the United Nations Conference on the Human Environment (Stockholm Declaration), (1972).

to protect the global Earth environment or the environment of one's own marine backyard.

4 Law from a Governance Perspective

4.1 *Introduction to Law*

The question for this section is how law is relevant to the structures and processes; ideals and standards; and substance of governance instruments. This question demands, initially, an introduction of 'law' in the context of this study. On the one hand, 'law' is eligible as (social) science, as per section 3.1. Knowledge about law certainly informs governance as one of multiple inputs and provides input to enlightenment (how humans within and across nations organize relations by law), orientation (the law relevant to certain topics such as fisheries or the law setting out societal goals), and values (knowledge about law may impact the desire to maintain those laws). Knowledge about law may further provide input to problem framing (whether the problem is the law, or the law poses a barrier to, or may facilitate responses to, the problem) and as input to the design and evaluation of a range of different policy options (such as different alternative laws).

On the other hand, and primarily, this study approaches law, on its own terms, from the perspective of the three governance components.[204] 'Law,' as per this study, means formal norms—norms that regulate and order behavior, authority, and formal governance processes, as will be further explained.[205] Formal norms include international norms that regulate relations between states, between states and international organizations, and (occasionally) between states and individuals. Further, formal norms include national legal norms specific to each national legal system, which regulates and orders how the state is organized; the distribution of the areas, resources, and ecosystems

204 The multiple ways of approaching governance and law entail that approaching the governance–law interface may expose very different results depending on the approach. Three examples that approach governance and law in different ways, and that are more philosophical and theoretical compared with this study, are Colombi Ciacchi and von der Pfordten, "Exploring the relationship between law and governance: a proposal."; Lewis A Kornhauser, "Law as an achievement of governance," *Journal of Legal Philosophy* 47, no. 1 (2022): 1–23; and Pauline Westerman, "Governing by Goals: Governance as a Legal Style," *Legisprudence* 1, no. 1 (2007): 51–72.

205 Inspired by Luis Felipe López-Calva and Yongmei Zhou, *Governance and the law* (Washington, District of Columbia: World Bank Group 2017), 83. They conceptualize these roles for national law, yet this study has expanded on the roles' description to capture international law and has changed the order to fit the approach of this study.

over which the state has jurisdictional or sovereign rights; regulation of behavior; and the relations between the state and citizens, companies, and organizations. The formal norms in mind are widespread and state centric, rather than a pluralistic take that captures broader variations of norms, such as traditional and religious law, and cultural and social norms (which certainly also regulate and order behavior, authority, and (informal) governance processes).

The formal norms in mind could be legally binding or non-binding (e.g., soft law[206]). Law is further perceived as a social construction (or a collective fiction)[207] resulting from political choices rather than derived from an inherent universal morality.[208] On this assumption, law is not inherently good or bad but serves those purposes reflected in the political choices of the time of adoption or coming into existence.[209] Throughout history and currently, law has been and is used, in some regimes, as a tool of injustice, oppression, and stagnation, and in other regimes, as a tool of justice and promotion of broadly supported societal goals. Law may serve as a powerful tool to meet broadly supported governance goals yet may be an equally powerful tool for those seeking to resist or challenge the same goals.[210]

The mere existence of law does not lead to the intended effect. Law as written may remain unimplemented (or untranslated), selectively implemented, translated to something different, and even impossible to implement.[211] Some

---

206 On soft and hard law, see, for example, Dinah Shelton, "Soft law," in *Routledge Handbook of International Law*, ed. David Armstrong (London: Taylor & Francis, 2009): 68 and Lavanya Rajamani, "The 2015 Paris Agreement: Interplay Between Hard, Soft and Non-Obligations," *Journal of Environmental Law* 28, no. 2 (2016): 337–58.

207 Yuval N. Harari, *Sapiens: A brief history of humankind* (New York: Harper 2015).

208 Woolaston, *Ecological Vulnerability: The Law and Governance of Human–Wildlife Relationships*: "Classical writers of legal theory, such as John Austin, H. L. A. Hart and Ronald Dworkin have long debated the existence of a definition of law and whether one is even necessary. One major point of contention is whether law has natural or positivist foundations, that is, whether law is derived from a 'higher' source and is based on an inherent, universal morality or whether law is a social construction that is only loosely associated with morality," 10.

209 Somewhat similar to political choices, but more elaborate, von der Pfordten in Colombi and von der Pfordten approaches the aim of law as "the mediation between possibly contrary, conflicting concerns." Colombi Ciacchi and von der Pfordten, "Exploring the relationship between law and governance: a proposal," 158.

210 López-Calva and Zhou, *Governance and the law*.

211 López-Calva and Zhou, *Governance and the law*. The question of the law as written versus the law as right, which could also be framed as a question of the rule of law, see Ruti Teitel, "Transitional Jurisprudence: The Role of Law in Political Transformation," *Yale L.J.* 106 (1996): 2009–2080.

reasons for law being hard or impossible to implement could be the existence of conflicting laws or an institutional culture or purpose in conflict with the law; a lack of knowledge, competence, or resources; or resistance to the law.

Inspired by López-Calva and Zhou, this study similarly suggests that law serves three governance roles in modern states.[212] The first role is to order power through establishing and distributing legal authority and power, or ways of using legal authority and power, among state actors, between a state and its citizens, between states, and between states and regional and international organizations.[213] This role will be discussed in the section on how law is relevant to governance structures. The second role is to order governance processes, including negotiating processes where policies, regulations, and individual decisions are made, and contestation processes "by providing the substantive and procedural tools needed to promote accountability, resolve disputes peacefully, and change the rules,"[214] which will be dealt with in the section on the relevance of law to governance processes. The third role is that of ordering the behavior of individuals, organizations, or states, which the section on the relevance of law to the substance of governance instruments will discuss.[215]

4.2 *Relevance of Law to Governance Structures and Processes*

4.2.1 Governance Structures

As per section 2.2, governance structures are partitioned into units, entailing a risk of fragmentation, which may be prevented. The relevance of law to governance structures is evident in how law defines formal governance structures and partition them into units, as evident in the first role of law of ordering (legal) authority and power.

The ordering of (legal) authority and power is recorded in mandates. Mandates include mandates given to a ministry, a directorate, or a regional or international organization, set out in statutes or other foundational documents, instructions, regulations, and conventions, if not implicitly through the establishment of an institution or organization. These countless mandates further reflect multiple units of governance. The mandates that set out the institutional or formal structure of governance reflect legal authority or power. Legal power

212 López-Calva and Zhou, *Governance and the law*, 83. They conceptualize these roles for national law, yet this study has expanded on the roles' description to capture international law. The numbering of the roles is different to that of López-Calva and Zhou.

213 Ibid, 83.

214 Ibid, 83. This role is expanded compared with the role of López-Calva and Zhou, which only captures contestation processes.

215 Ibid, 83.

is vested in states as sovereign units within which peoples are organized.[216] By the law of sovereignty, states have terrestrial and marine entitlements and legal and jurisdictional power over territories and waters, activities, and citizens.[217]

The formal legal authority of states forms the basis for (re)distributing access to resources and marine spaces to private persons, economic entities, and local communities (under national law). The legal governance structure perspectives are different from perspectives focusing on, for example, economy, relations, or (real) power (such as military power, power of size, power of alliances) and interests, as well as those focusing on interactions. Moreover, governance approaches focusing on multilevel management perspectives or multiple actors may marginalize or exclude the legal power perspective, as it is characteristic of one legally empowered kind of actor (sovereign states), in this sense state centric. Nonetheless, as Biermann et al. provides, from a governance perspective, "there is general agreement that authority and steering are its [governance's] two core components."[218] Therefore, the role of law in ordering legal authority and power is a key perspective to the institutional or formal structures of governance. Law could even be perceived as providing the infrastructure of governance,[219] and governance structures may even be perceived as legal structures. Ruhl et al. explain how a legal system is:

> the system that creates, implements, and enforces formal rules governing society ... [including] both the institutions tasked with creating and applying legal rules, as well as legal instruments, such as laws and regulations.[220]

Thus, the legal system of Ruhl comprises the formal rules governing society, including both institutional and instrumental elements. If formal rules and legal instruments are interpreted widely, to include policies (e.g., as soft law[221]), the legal system of Ruhl captures vital parts of the formal governance structures

216 Montevideo Convention on the Rights and Duties of States, adopted 26 December 1933, entered into force 26 December 1934, 1761 UNTS.

217 UNCLOS, art 56, and art 77. Ian Brownlie, *Principles of public international law*, 7th ed. (Oxford: Oxford University Press, 2008), 289, describes the principles of state jurisdiction over territory and the permanent population.

218 Biermann et al., "Global Goal Setting for Improving National Governance and Policy," 75.

219 As articulated by Vonintsoa Rafaly at the IUCN IEL Colloquium Joensuu 2023.

220 Ruhl, Cosens, and Soininen, "Resilience of Legal Systems: Toward Adaptive Governance," 510.

221 On soft and hard law, see, for example, Shelton, "Soft law" and Rajamani, "The 2015 Paris Agreement: Interplay Between Hard, Soft and Non-Obligations."

that this study articulates (or a governance system, although not in the sense of system theorists as per section 2.1).[222] This highlights the relevance of law to the formal governance structures (unlike the informal structures such as certain networks).

The possibilities and options vested in the legal authority perspective extend beyond the existing institutions. While existing institutions reflect formalization (if not cementation) of political choices as per current and previous choices, the legal authority empowers relevant actors to create new institutions, to redesign or transform existing structures, and to phase out or wind up institutions (and what they manage or regulate) as they see fit. The practical possibilities of powering change are certainly a question. Once created, structures of institutions may not easily be revised (such as to reflect different partitioning). Investments made in an existing institution (e.g., through mandates, commitment, funds, employment, and beyond) and the outcome it may have produced may become a self-sustaining force. Further, institutional choices and fine regulation of topics adhering to existing partitioning add to the challenge.[223]

Therefore, existing institutions may reflect self-imposed restrictions on multiple states and rules of the game for multiple actors. While in the last decade new ocean paradigms have been launched in policies and research,[224] including maritime security, blue economy, ocean health, and ocean justice, the legal institutions at large remain unchanged. Some recent international exceptions are the High Level Panel for a Sustainable Ocean Economy,[225] and any new institutions that may be established under the High Seas Biodiversity Treaty.[226] Moreover, while many institutions remains unchanged, the actions, interactions, and impact made by them could certainly evolve, reflecting the evolution of the substance of ocean governance as per the approach of this study.

---

222 The legal system of Ruhl further resembles the hierarchical governance mode of Kooiman, which comprises both the legal and the policy arena, see Kooiman, *Governing as Governance*, 123. Kooiman sees hierarchical governance as opposed to the modes of self-governance and co-governance.

223 Furthermore, narratives, assumptions, and bias may evolve, inviting for approaching the units as regimes (e.g., Young, "Regime Interaction in Creating, Implementing and Enforcing International Law," 86) which is, however, out-of-scope of this study.

224 Bueger and Mallin, "Blue Paradigms: Understanding the Intellectual Revolution in Global Ocean Politics."

225 "About the Ocean Panel https://oceanpanel.org/about-ocean-panel/," World Resources Institute, 2023.

226 Agreement under the United Nations Convention on the Law of the Sea on the conservation and sustainable use of marine biological diversity of areas beyond national jurisdiction, adopted 19 June 2023.

Now that the relevance of law to the governance structures and units have been discussed, the question remains of law's relevance to the risk of fragmentation and ways of preventing fragmentation. The partitioning of formal governance by law in mandates is, in one sense, the very cause of fragmentation, as it is the definition and providing of a mandate that separates the mandate from the larger whole (the exclusive powers of sovereign states). From another perspective, the granting of a mandate that combines the power of different states, such as combining states' efforts on global plastics pollution into one instrument, may be seen as a way of preventing fragmentated (single states') effort. Therefore, law may both create fragmentation, by defining and issuing mandates, and prevent fragmentation, by defining mandates that complements existing partitioning. This illustrates the importance of justifying an argument of fragmentation (or integration) and its limits.

4.2.2 Governance Processes

Through establishing the mandates for state actors (the first role of law for governance), law explicates the separation of state power and the responsibilities of different agencies and government branches and international organizations. The question now is how law is relevant to the governance processes that section 2.2 has described.

Legal requirements and rules exist for governance processes or phases of it, reflecting the second role of law of defining or framing formal governance processes. Requirements of governance processes could require the appointment of someone responsible for conducting the process in a certain way or at a certain frequency. The OSPAR Convention requires assessments of the quality status of the marine environment of the northeast Atlantic to be made at regular intervals.[227] Another example relevant to the knowledge gathering and analysis phase is the Espoo Convention, which requires environmental impacts to be assessed prior to the planning of certain activities.[228] Further, relevant to this process phase, duties to gather knowledge (such as by requiring environmental impact assessments as per the Espoo Convention example, or assessments of economic or administrative character) as well as providing legal authority to gather knowledge exist. Law may grant rights to obtain or obligations to produce knowledge, such as environmental information, or to consult with certain

227 Convention for the Protection of the Marine Environment of the North-East Atlantic (OSPAR), adopted 22 September 1992, entered into force 25 March 1998, 2354 UNTS 67, Art 6.

228 Convention on Environmental Impact Assessment in a Transboundary Context (Espoo Convention), adopted 25 February 1991, entered into force 10 September 1997, 1989 UNTS 309.

stakeholders (such as local communities, indigenous peoples, and economic actors). With respect to the decision-making phase, law may provide authority or mandate to design and adopt policies and regulations, and tools and strategies, including strategic and individual decision-making. Legal requirements could also apply to the implementation (or translation) or monitoring phase.

Beyond setting out the rules, law provides terminology, structure, and formality for naming and ordering things, for detailing the order of things and for creating and for challenging and arguing for and against this order.[229] For example, the EU Maritime Spatial Planning Directive provides terminology and a concept of marine spatial plans, the rules on how EU states should make marine spatial plans, which are complemented by national rules on such plans at state level.[230] The rules about lawmaking processes would often subject to constitutions, defining different roles or process steps of governments and parliaments.[231]

Various kinds of formal governance processes exist beyond those policy-making and lawmaking processes that section 2.2 has described. While policy-making and lawmaking processes could be characterized as creative or negotiation processes,[232] where different interests are negotiated to create a policy or law, contestation processes are another type of governance processes. As per López-Calva and Zhou, by contestation processes law provides the substantive and procedural tools needed to promote accountability, resolve disputes peacefully, and change the rules.[233]

Therefore, law defines certain contestation processes, such as enforcement processes. Institutions and instruments of legal enforcement (such as courts within a national legal system) facilitate that certain claimants (such as economic actors or indigenous peoples) under certain conditions may pursue certain claims (such as entitlement to areas or ecosystem components/resources) related to their legal position (such as entitlement to a license or right of non-infringement). These institutions and instruments may ensure that some decisions meet certain standards and that legal positions are not hampered unless

229 Directive 2014/89/EU of the European Parliament and of the Council of 23 July 2014 establishing a framework for maritime spatial planning, OJ L 257, 28.8.2014, 135–145.

230 For example, as evident in section 12 of the preamble of the directive.

231 For example, Josh Chafetz, *Congress's Constitution: Legislative Authority and the Separation of Powers* (New Haven, CT: Yale University Press, 2017).

232 Inspired by, Christophe Dupont and Guy-Oliver Faure, "The negotiation process," *International negotiation* (1991): 40–57; William Zartman, "Negotiation as a joint decision-making process," *Journal of Conflict Resolution* 21, no. 4 (1977): 619–38.

233 López-Calva and Zhou, *Governance and the law*, 83.

they follow assigned procedures. These mechanisms therefore strengthen existing legal positions.

Through the existence of independent (national) legal systems and by qualifying claims and claimants, law further excludes other interests and actors from contestation processes. For example, where no right of nature is conceptualized in law or where non-interference with global ecosystems is not an obligation, contestation on rights of nature or obligations of non-interference with global ecosystems are excluded by law.

Changing existing legal positions (rights and obligations) through the lawmaking and law-revising processes is demanding and time-consuming and may meet resistance from politicians, stakeholders, and those privileged by existing legal positions. Therefore, changes to governance instruments and decisions, which have or may have implications for the legal positions of legal and natural persons, may be demanding, time-consuming, or hindered. In this sense, current law (or those privileged by it) poses a potential barrier to the responsiveness or adaptivity of governance. Nonetheless, law plays a constitutive or foundational role of defining or framing multiple formal governance processes.

4.3 *Relevance of Law in Ideals and Standards of Governance*

Now the relevance of law will be approached from the perspective of governance ideals and standards. Law is often associated with certain ideals and standards. As per section 4.2, lawmaking processes are a particular kind of governance process. As per Fukuyama, lawmaking processes are designed to include procedures "guaranteeing that the law corresponds to a broad social consensus on basic values."[234] Lawmaking processes are further designed to meet certain ideals and standards, including thoroughness and transparency. When lawmaking processes involve consulting stakeholders and parliamentary adoption, governance instruments and decisions formalized in law meet certain standards of participatory processes and legitimacy. These ideals and standards could, at least in principle, also be designed and built into governance processes resulting in something different than a legal instrument, such as a plan, policy, or strategic decision.

Further, law is also strongly associated with some other ideals and standards, such as predictability, finality, and enforceability, which are less relevant to policies and strategies. Conceptualizations of the 'rule of law' captures such ideals and standards.[235] Fukuyama conceptualizes the rule of law not to be

234 Francis Fukuyama, "Transitions to the Rule of Law," *Journal of democracy* 21, no. 1 (2010): 33–44, 34.

235 Noting, however, that this concept and related concepts have developed differently in dif-

bound by a specific substantive understanding but "as a set of rules of behavior, reflecting a broad consensus within the society, that is binding on even the most powerful political actors …"[236] As per López-Calva and Zhou, the rule of law "at its core requires that government officials and citizens be bound by and act consistently with the law."[237] Teitel similarly understands it as adherence to settled laws.[238] This bindingness and adherence to law is what paves the way for predictability, finality, and enforceability.[239]

Versions of the rule of law have moved beyond predictability, finality, and enforceability to focus on property rights and contract enforcement, or the modern Western understanding of human rights, which includes equal rights for women and racial and ethnic minorities.[240] A report of the UN Secretary-General on the rule of law and transitional justice in conflict and post-conflict societies uses a definition that includes such elements:

> For the United Nations, the rule of law refers to a principle of governance in which all persons, institutions and entities, public and private, including the State itself, are accountable to laws that are publicly promulgated, equally enforced and independently adjudicated, and which are consistent with international human rights norms and standards. It requires, as well, measures to ensure adherence to the principles of supremacy of law, equality before the law, accountability to the law, fairness in the application of the law, separation of powers, participation in decision-making, legal certainty, avoidance of arbitrariness and procedural and legal transparency.[241]

This definition of the rule of law may trigger many important questions relevant to ocean governance, such as whether current structures, processes or

---

ferent contexts, or, as per, Machiko Kanetake and André Nollkaemper, *The rule of law at the national and international levels: contestations and deference*, v. 56 (Oxford,Portland, Oregon: Hart Publishing Ltd, 2016), the concept allows for flexibility, national diversity, and pluralism.

236 Francis Fukuyama, *Political Order and Political Decay: From the Industrial Revolution to the Globalization of Democracy* (London: Profile Books, 2014), 19.

237 López-Calva and Zhou, *Governance and the law*, 83.

238 Teitel, "Transitional Jurisprudence: The Role of Law in Political Transformation."

239 Separation of powers within a state is further relevant to this, and a key topic for the rule of law, yet is out of scope of this study.

240 Fukuyama, *Political Order and Political Decay: From the Industrial Revolution to the Globalization of Democracy*.

241 UN Secretary-General S/2004/616, *The rule of law and transitional justice in conflict and post-conflict societies*, United Nations (New York, 2004).

instruments of ocean governance are fair, equal, and just.[242] In literature on ocean governance, some use the rule of law seemingly in the procedural sense, focusing on predictability.[243]

Formalizing the outcome of governance processes as law has certain benefits relevant to ocean governance (and beyond), as captured by the rule of law concept. These include avoiding arbitrariness and ensuring that governance is transparent or legitimate. The entrenchment of law, setting strong requirements to changing it, may provide credibility over time by guarding against shifts in preferences.[244] Like any ideal, formalization in law may also be perceived as disadvantageous. Once adopted, law could be demanding to change, perceived as cementation of choices (which is only disadvantageous so long as what is cemented in law is deemed disadvantageous), and institutional arrangements may develop around them, making them even more demanding to change. While legal instruments may attempt to grasp today what is relevant tomorrow, unforeseen circumstances and consequences and changing political preferences may lead to a desire for change—of processes, partitioning, legal instruments, or decisions based on them. For these and other reasons, law will have to strike a balance between the concerns of inflexibility (for reasons of accountability, predictability, ensuring adherence and finality, avoiding arbitrariness and more) and concerns of flexibility (providing a margin of appreciation, discrepancy, delegation of powers, responsiveness, or adaptivity). Inevitably, these sets of concerns of inflexibility and flexibility are contradictory. Yet, as per Bohman, "(a)daptive governance measures in law does not have to entail unpredictable laws or uncertainty."[245] Further, as per Platjouw and Soininen:

---

242 Some literature that deals with these topics include Bennett et al., "Blue growth and blue justice: Ten risks and solutions for the ocean economy;" Campbell et al., "From Blue Economy to Blue Communities: reorienting aquaculture expansion for community wellbeing;" Irini Papanicolopulu ed, *Gender and the Law of the Sea* (Boston: Boston: BRILL, 2019); Greg Severinsen, "Oceans reform in Aotearoa New Zealand: a just transition?," *Policy Quarterly* 17, no. 3 (2021): 45–53. On the normative limits of legitimate political change in the midst of transformation, see Teitel, "Transitional Jurisprudence: The Role of Law in Political Transformation," 2018.

243 Froukje Maria Platjouw and Niko Soininen, "Reconciling the rule of law with adaptive regulation of marine ecosystems—Challenges and opportunities for the Arctic and beyond," *Marine policy* 110 (2019): 103726.

244 López-Calva and Zhou, *Governance and the law*.

245 Brita Bohman, "Regulatory control of adaptive fisheries: Reflections on the implementation of the landing obligation in the EU common fisheries policy," *Marine Policy* 110 (2019): 103557.

> good examples [exist] that allow reconciling different rule of law values, including coherence, predictability, stability and legal certainty, public participation, and accountability, with the need for adaptive regulation and governance. Adaptivity may be built into the legal design of aquaculture or fisheries regulation, adaptivity may be fostered through iterative planning and licensing systems, and also the law-making process itself may be adaptive.[246]

Thus, Platjouw and Soininen argue that rule of law and adaptivity could be reconciled. Arguably, such reconciliation already exists to some extent in the flexibility and margin of appreciation provided in existing legal instruments. Further, there are limits to such arguments. On one hand, reconciling rule of law and adaptivity may be possible, for example, within the limits of a single legal instrument concerning some pre-defined scenarios. For example, along what Platjouw and Soininen suggest, one could envision aquaculture regulation granting time-limited licenses, providing for licenses to be changed or withdrawn dependent on, for example, changes in the environment or the environmental footprint of aquaculture.

On the other hand, it is challenging to imagine how legal design could accommodate rule of law values, such as predictability, finality, and enforceability and adaptivity in the face of multiple ways of considering the complicatedness of competing and potentially conflicting scientific and nonscientific inputs relevant to policies and regulation, the multiple policy and regulatory alternatives that scientific evidence may give rise to, and the demand for political anchoring or legitimacy of changes or adaptations to policies or regulations. For example, if one imagines a scientific input, such as increased eutrophication in a marine area, which policy options could it give rise to? For example, the restriction of nearby conventional agriculture or nearby conventional aquaculture, or the improvement of nearby wastewater treatment facilities? Or perhaps ocean warming is enhancing the effects of eutrophication,[247] to which uncertainty is attached and which raises the question of which activities or behavior lead to ocean warming, which likely is all activities that has a carbon footprint, which may make the issue a global one, unlike a local one.

---

246 Platjouw and Soininen, "Reconciling the rule of law with adaptive regulation of marine ecosystems—Challenges and opportunities for the Arctic and beyond," 3.

247 Jessica Pazzaglia et al., "Does Warming Enhance the Effects of Eutrophication in the Seagrass Posidonia oceanica?" Original Research, *Frontiers in Marine Science* 7 (2020): fmars-07-564805.

In such complicated cases, this study highlights the role of the inherently cross-sectoral governments or head of states. They may deal with all these issues, for example, requiring reduced emissions from all of agriculture, aquaculture, and wastewater treatment, whether within the margin of appreciation of these instruments or following a process of change of these instruments. They may further negotiate with neighboring or multiple states on the reduction of relevant emissions such as CO_2-emissions. The potential for adaptivity reconciled with rule of law values at government or head of state level is vast.

A question related to the justification and limits of the rule of law ideal, in the meaning of legal certainty and predictability, is in whose interests is it to have legal certainty or, at the opposite end, flexibility? Some examples of economic actors promoting legal certainty or predictability are fishers relying on a quota, having invested in vessel and gear with the quota in mind, or investors planning for investments in low trophic species harvest and production. These actors wish to limit their economic risk, which legal certainty and predictability could provide for. Yet, other actors and interests including other interests of these fishers and investors could equally benefit from legal certainty and predictability to limit environmental risk—the risk that the functions of the ecosystems are not maintained sufficiently to enable resource outtake. In theory, legal certainty and predictability could, on the one hand, serve the interest of economic entities in facilitating a steady economic regime. On the other hand, legal certainty and predictability could, at least in theory, serve environmental interests, for example, ensuring the protection of ocean health that the fishers and investors and beyond depend on. Yet, as the present status and trends of the marine environment clearly indicate its continuous deterioration, one could plausibly argue that current environmental protection in law remains theoretical. This raises the question of the law as written versus the law as right, which could also be framed as a question of the rule of law,[248] which, however, is out of the scope of this study.

4.4 *Relevance of Law to the Substance of Governance Instruments*

As per section 2.3, the substantive instruments of governance are policies and regulations. The approach aligns with a third role of law of ordering behavior. Law as an instrument of governance sets out rules about how individuals, organizations and companies, and states shall behave, in regulations and policies, conventions and treaties, and as customary law. Therefore, the ordering of behavior is often recorded by regulations and policies. The regulations and policies are numerous, reflecting multiple partitions of governance.

248 Teitel, "Transitional Jurisprudence: The Role of Law in Political Transformation."

From a perspective of law that embraces any formal law, including soft-law instruments, policies and regulations could both be labeled as law. Therefore, the substance of governance instruments aligns with an approach to law embracing soft- and hard-law instruments. Accordingly, the instruments of governance equal the instruments of law (under the soft-law approach) and the substance of laws could be mapped using each of the approaches to the substance of governance, as per section 2.4 (where; what and how; who; why). Certainly, investigations of governance instruments could also go beyond studying legal instruments. For example, Rudd et al. investigate "Ocean Ecosystem-Based Management Mandates and Implementation in the North Atlantic," by using a multilevel approach studying political mandate, legislative structure, and nonregulatory implementing policy.[249]

While the governance perspective resembles soft-law approaches, some governance and research questions rather attract a hard-law approach. Notably, in ocean governance, permission to interfere with ecosystems (such as emission permits, resource use and outtake, new constructions, and area use) would often require a hard legal basis, as would distribution of, and obtaining, individual rights to ecosystem components. One may ask why interference with ecosystems requires a hard legal basis. One explanation is that by the logic of sovereignty, territorial and jurisdictional entitlements are distributed between states. Further, through the social contract between a state and its citizens, the state is responsible for, and is granted, authority to manage and interfere with ecosystems, whether by public entities or private companies and the details of which are normally positively authorized or regulated by hard law.[250] This explains the usefulness of a hard law focus in ocean governance.

Which legal instruments are relevant for ecosystem and ocean governance depend on how the substance matter of ocean governance is perceived. If determined by their geographical scope of application, international and national legal instruments would often define the geographical scope to which they apply. UNCLOS is a key international legal instrument that divides the ocean into different zones and sets out states' rights and obligations relevant to each geographical zone.[251] Other international legal instruments applicable in ocean

249 Murray A. Rudd et al., "Ocean Ecosystem-Based Management Mandates and Implementation in the North Atlantic," Original Research, *Frontiers in Marine Science* 5 (2018): Article 458.

250 Reflecting certain interpretations of the principle of legality in private law or property law contexts, see for example, Jason N. E. Varuhas, "The principle of legality," *C.L.J.* 79, no. 3 (2020): 578–614.

251 As reflected in Parts II, V, VI, VII, XI of UNCLOS.

areas include the High Seas Biodiversity Treaty,[252] which applies to the high seas—the ocean areas beyond national jurisdiction. Some national legal instruments applicable in ocean areas are the marine management plans of Norway and the Marine Resources Act of Norway.[253] The geographical approach reflects the area that these legal instruments seek to govern but does not necessarily regulate those activities against which an area needs protection.

Under the 'what and how' approach as per section 2.4, which legal instruments are relevant to ocean governance depends on the perception of ocean governance. If it is perceived as the management of maritime activities, the legal instruments of relevance are those that regulate existing or emerging activities, such as conventions and regulations of shipping, fishing, aquaculture, or offshore renewable energy. If ocean governance is perceived as those activities that interfere with marine ecosystems (which these ecosystems need protection against), a delimitation of relevant instruments is demanded, as most maritime and land based activities interfere with marine ecosystems, such as inducing some pollution, waste, or GHG emissions. If the criteria or the selection approach reflects the main threats to the global marine environment, the instruments relevant to overfishing, increased use of space, climate change, and non-native species (which the IPBES 2019 report identifies as the five main threats)[254] could be relevant. If the selection focuses on local pressures, the relevant legal instruments will depend on what these local pressures are. The selection could also capture certain legal instruments that may shed light on how international or national law targets global, regional, national, and local pressures. Further, the selection could focus on indirect drivers common to all or most pressures on the global marine environment, such as, as per the IPBES report, "a variety of economic, political and social factors, including global trade and the spatial decoupling of production from consumption."[255]

---

252 Agreement under the United Nations Convention on the Law of the Sea on the conservation and sustainable use of marine biological diversity of areas beyond national jurisdiction, adopted 19 June 2023.

253 Integrated Management Plan for the Norwegian Marine Areas. Report nr. 20 to the Storting (2019–2020); Marine Resources Act, "Lov om forvaltning av viltlevande marine ressursar (havressurslova) LOV-2008-06-06-37," (Oslo: Lovdata, 2008).

254 Díaz et al., *IPBES 2019: Summary for policymakers of the global assessment report on biodiversity and ecosystem services (summary for policy makers). IPBES Plenary at its seventh session (IPBES 7, Paris, 2019)*; E. S. Brondízio et al., *IPBES The global assessment report on biodiversity and ecosystem services, summary for policymakers, available at* https://www.ipbes.net/global-assessment IPBES (Bonn, Germany, 2019).

255 Díaz et al., *IPBES 2019: Summary for policymakers of the global assessment report on biodiversity and ecosystem services (summary for policy makers). IPBES Plenary at its seventh session (IPBES 7, Paris, 2019).*

Under the 'who' approach that targets relevant ocean governance actors and demands of those actors, different actors attract different legal instruments. The rights and obligations of coastal states are, for example, set out in UNCLOS.[256] Regulation of coastal communities is subject to any national or local regulation of such communities. Economic actors, as maritime industries are often organized, are regulated by corporate legislation of various countries.

The 'why' approach targets the purpose or societal objective of a governance instrument. Legal instruments are instruments for articulating societal objectives, following a law-making process. While policies, plans, and strategies may discuss societal objectives in more detail, hard legal instruments are often characterized by providing short formulations of purpose or objectives in the legal text (while the non-legally binding preamble or *travaux préparatoires*[257] may elaborate on the purposes and objectives). The regulation of behavior, authority, or formal governance processes may rarely be derived from these objectives, as such regulation would require more specificity for example, for reasons of predictability. The purposes and objectives of legal instruments are nonetheless relevant to the interpretation of other provisions that regulate behavior, authority, and formal governance processes.[258]

5 Perspectives Provided to Ocean Governance Research

The question is now what this theoretical framework has to offer for ocean governance research. Section 5.1 will offer some perspectives from the study to some of the ideals and standards of ocean governance that traverses the governance–science interface: cross-sectoral, integrated, and holistic approaches; the ecosystem approach; and responsiveness and adaptability. Section 5.2 draws conclusions from the study including on the emerging field of the study of ocean governance.

256 As reflected, for example, in Parts II, IV and V, UNCLOS.

257 The documents evidencing the negotiation, discussions, and drafting of a final treaty text.

258 For international treaties, this is reflected in art 31 of the Vienna Convention on the Law of Treaties, 1155 UNTS 331. For national regulation, consult the doctrinal method of each state.

5.1 *Ideals and Standards of Ocean Governance Traversing the Governance–Science Interface*

5.1.1 Cross-Sectoral, Integrated, and Holistic Approaches Facing Partitioning

The question for this section is what the theoretical framework has to offer to the cross-sectoral, integrated, and holistic approaches in ocean governance, which transcend the governance–science interface. The governance perspective has unpacked how governance structures (by mandates) and governance instruments (by scope of application) entails a division or partitioning of governance into units. The ultimate justification of partitioning could be, for example, to construct manageable units avoiding that each unit covers too diverse topics, too many obligations, or requiring too diverse expertise. The justification of how-to partition could vary, yet each perspective will be limited.

One common demand to practiced ocean governance by ocean governance scholarship is the demand for cross-sectoral management of marine activities. One example is "while current management is largely fragmented, with most sectors managed by individual laws, agencies, or regulatory regimes, there are calls for integrated, cross-sectoral management approaches to achieve EBM [ecosystem-based management]."[259] This example challenges the current partition of national instruments and organizational units. Yet, it does not discuss how it imagines partition to be redesigned (one cross-sectoral management regime, one cross-sectoral agency, and a cross-sectoral law?) and how to accommodate those purposes substantiating the current design and those limitations inherent in the alternative perspective. Combining laws, agencies, and regulatory regimes may have advantages or be appropriate for some purposes but may be less appropriate for others, such as those which the partition is based on.

The marine sectors have some common interfaces, such as operating at sea, which justifies some kind of integration, coordination, or consultation, to the extent operations overlap in time and space, to account for the interests of different activities.[260] However, on the other hand, there are clear differences between marine sectors. For example, it appears inappropriate to co-manage the issues of how to distribute cod quotas between countries, which tourists a country would want to attract, and which offshore renewable energy sources to

---

259 Dane H. Klinger et al., "The mechanics of blue growth: Management of oceanic natural resource use with multiple, interacting sectors," *Marine Policy* 87 (2018): 356–62, 356, references omitted in the quote.

260 Lena Schøning, "More or Less Integrated Ocean Management: Multiple Integrated Approaches and Two Norms," *Ocean Development & International Law* 51, no. 2 (2019): 95–115.

prioritize. Bilateral distribution of cod quotas could, for example, more appropriately be co-managed with other fisheries or bilateral affairs between those two countries. Which tourists a country wants to attract could be co-planned with which infrastructure the country wants to facilitate, whether airports, cruise ports, or railroad tracks. Which offshore renewable energy source to prioritize could appropriately be dealt with in combination with the issue of which mix of energy sources and related energy infrastructure and energy consumption a country wants to facilitate. Thus, cross-sectoral management of tourism, fisheries, offshore energy production, and other marine sectors is appropriate for some purposes but not all.

This study has shown how no partition or division would account for all of the different perspectives that governance demands. Thus, some topics or perspectives will always be governed across other divisions, topics, or perspectives or be governed in a 'fragmented' way. Therefore, inherent in any governance structure partitioned into units is a risk of fragmentation. Therefore, this study suggests that the calls for cross-sectoral, integrated, or holistic approaches should be justified and their purposes specified. How do these calls consider non-partitioning or redesigned partitioning of governance institutions, processes, and instruments and for which purposes? Do they ask for less partitioning or redesigned partitioning, in merit, structure, or both?

One common reason to justify cross-sectoral approaches is that it could increase the attention given to cumulative environmental impacts.[261] The impacts on the environment of the different marine sectors, such as fisheries, shipping, and tourism, throughout their life cycles,[262] include local waste, physical disturbance, use of space (at sea and on land), resource outtake, global pollution, and CO_2 impacts. Thus, the impacts vary in scale and nature, some traceable at sea, some on land, and some only in aggregation (such as CO_2), if traceable at all. These impacts could be perceived as a result of the demand for the activity (such as fisheries meeting a demand for food), of the regulation of fisheries throughout their life cycle, or of the available substitutional goods and services (such as other sources of food and employment). Considering these circumstances, the question remains whether any of these impacts, such as from fisheries, would be appropriately governed in combination with impacts from shipping, tourism, and other marine sectors. While cumulative

261 For example, Charles, "People, oceans and scale: governance, livelihoods and climate change adaptation in marine social–ecological systems;" Kelly et al., "Investigating options on how to address cumulative impacts in marine spatial planning;" Josh Martin, "A Transnational Law of the Sea," *Chicago journal of international law* 21, no. 2 (2021): 419–75.

262 Schøning, "The Contribution of Integrated Marine Policies to Marine Environmental Protection: The Case of Norway," 26.

environmental impacts may be necessary to provide information about the environmental status of a certain marine space, this does not necessarily mean that the activities operating in a certain marine area should be governed in integration.

These cross-sectoral examples illustrate that while partitioning is necessary, how to partition is demanding as inherent limitations exist in any approach. Ideally and theoretically speaking, plural crosscutting perspectives could be useful, as each would be limited, even those deeming themselves holistic, integrated, coherent, or cross-sectoral. What is integrated from one perspective, such as managing in combination activities using the same marine space, may not be integrated from the perspective of environmental impacts of one sector. Practically speaking, plural crosscutting policies and regulations, strategies, and tools could be envisioned; however, crosscutting institutional structures may conflict with a concern for structural integration as well as the desire for lean institutions and organizations.

While discussing partition relevant to ocean governance and even ecosystem governance, the question emerges why do we have (and do we need) 'ocean governance' or 'ecosystem governance'? Are these useful ways of partitioning governance? Often, it is human interference, activities, or behavior that need to be governed or drive the need for governance, which these two terms do not convey very well, at least in a semantic sense. Ultimately, it depends on how we define ocean governance and ecosystem governance and the purpose of the term or concept, including what we leave out when we deem something as, for example, ocean governance. If, for example, responding to the main threats to the global marine ecosystems is the purpose,[263] the threat posed by overfishing could perhaps be appropriately dealt with as fisheries management (assuming it captures the drivers of overfishing). The increasing demand for marine space may, for example, be appropriately dealt with as marine space management, capturing those activities demanding marine space, the governing agents of

263 Bernal et al., "Chapter 54. Overall Assessment of Human Impacts on the Oceans." identify seven main pressures on the global marine environment: (1) climate change (including ocean acidification); (2) fishing and harvesting; (3) marine pollution; (4) increased demand for marine space; (5) underwater noise; (6) interfering structures; and (7) non-native species (as spread by shipping, aquaculture, and marine debris). This taxonomy of the main pressures is roughly similar to the five direct drivers in the global marine environment of Díaz et al., *IPBES 2019: Summary for policymakers of the global assessment report on biodiversity and ecosystem services (summary for policy makers). IPBES Plenary at its seventh session (IPBES 7, Paris, 2019)*: (1) fisheries and other harvesting of marine organisms; (2) change in area use on land and at sea, including development of infrastructure and aquaculture in the coastal zone; (3) climate change; (4) pollution and waste; and (5) invasive and alien species.

these activities, or the human behavior driving the need for those activities. The threats of climate change and long-range transported pollution, which primarily stem from both land-based and maritime activities, may be more appropriately dealt with as 'ocean and terrestrial' governance. As all three problems stem from human activities, addressing them as human governance may sometimes be more appropriate than ecosystem or ocean governance. Nonetheless, ocean governance and ecosystem governance may be appropriate for some purposes, yet not for all, and, arguably, any choice of concept should be substantiated in order to clarify the purpose and thus the limitations inherent in any approach.[264]

Therefore, this study challenges calls to interconnect or integrate policies, regulations, or institutions and organizations to justify why, for example, a more interconnected or integrated way of organizing or regulating leads to a more desirable result or outcome (rather than letting interconnections or integration be the preferred outcome). Furthermore, 'fragmentation' as a way of representing problems[265] should be justified, considering, for example, advantages and disadvantages of current partitioning of governance units and instruments.

Calls for interconnections, integration, cross-sectoral, and other perspectives often underscore cooperation or interaction across institutions and organizations. Certainly, justifiable reasons exist to cooperate and interact, such as, to avoid overlaps, draw synergies, and not undermine the work of another, which may counteract disadvantages of fragmentation. While perspectives studying cooperation and interactions are necessary, and all perspectives may complement one another, this study wishes to emphasize operation (unlike the cooperation) and action (unlike the interaction). As per Cosens, we "need to go beyond producing knowledge about our world to generating wisdom about how to act within it."[266] If institutions and organizations are not appropriately and sufficiently acting to further ocean governance, increased interaction will arguably not take us there. For this reason, this study wishes to push for exploration and development of the substance or merit of ocean governance and the capacity to act.

---

264 A short reminder of the justification for theorizing ocean governance in this study is that it is emerging as a field of study on its own, and the current spotlight on ocean governance practices. The limits inherent in the approach includes that it investigates by theorizing three components of governance and the relevance of science and law to each component.

265 Bacchi, *Analysing policy: what's the problem represented to be?*

266 Cosens et al., "Governing complexity: Integrating science, governance, and law to manage accelerating in the commons."

5.1.2 The Ecosystem Approach in Ocean Governance

Aligning variants of the ecosystem approach with the approach to governance of this study makes some reflections relevant to ocean governance. Multiple interpretations of the ecosystem approach exist. Some would highlight certain management process phases (as Kelly et al.)[267] or presumed structural risks ('integrated management,' as per the Conference of Parties (COP) to the Convention on Biological Diversity (CBD) definition),[268] or certain ideals such as participation.[269] Definitions, principles, and literature on the ecosystem approach frequently refer to many of the same components that ocean governance captures (integrated management, participatory processes, monitoring, evaluation, and adaptation).[270] As per this framework, these components are generic to any type of governance or management; thus, rather than describing aspects of an ecosystem approach, ecosystem governance, or ecosystem-based management, they describe aspects of governance or management. The approach of this framework facilitates asking what remains of substance of the ecosystem approach when the process phases, the structural risks, and the ideals and standards that are generic to all kinds of governance (including tax issues) are kept outside.

According to the CBD COP decisions,[271] the ecosystem approach is "a strategy for the integrated management of land, water and living resources that promotes conservation and sustainable use in an equitable way."[272] In light of the approach of this study, the first part of this definition could be taken to refer to integrated processes or structures and the second part captures an objective that reflects one element of substance ('why').

267 Kelly et al., "Investigating options on how to address cumulative impacts in marine spatial planning."

268 Convention on Biodiversity COP 5 Decision V/6, source: https://www.cbd.int/decision/cop/?id=7148 (last accessed 4 April 2023).

269 For example, Augustin Berghöfer, Heidi Wittmer, and Felix Rauschmayer, "Stakeholder participation in ecosystem-based approaches to fisheries management: A synthesis from European research projects," *Marine policy* 32, no. 2 (2008) 243–253.

270 See, for example, the literature and sources referred to in this section 5.1.3.

271 Decisions made by COP under the Convention on Biological Diversity (CBD). For an overview of the COP decisions, see source: https://www.cbd.int/ecosystem/decisions.shtml (last accessed 25 April 2023). As held by Langlet and Rayfuse, "the definition and principles provided within the CBD regime remain a central articulation of the conceptual ideas of ecosystem-thinking," Langlet and Rayfuse, "The Ecosystem Approach in Ocean Planning and Governance: An Introduction," 2.

272 Convention on Biodiversity COP 7 Decision VII/11.

The Malawi principles serve as another interpretation of the ecosystem approach.[273] In "The Ecosystem Approach and the Search for An Objective and Content for the Concept of Holistic Ocean Governance," Kirk finds that three of these principles concern the decision-making (or governance) process, four of them are issues to be taken into consideration in decision-making, and four of them concern objectives.[274] The latter eight could accordingly be considered as aspects of governance substance as per this study.

For the purpose of the OSPAR Convention, the OSPAR Commission has defined the ecosystem approach as:

> the comprehensive integrated management of human activities based on the best available scientific knowledge about the ecosystem and its dynamics, in order to identify and take action on influences which are critical to the health of marine ecosystems, thereby achieving sustainable use of ecosystem goods and services and maintenance of ecosystem integrity.[275]

Aligned with this study, this definition includes both structural aspects, an ideal of best available science, and some substantive aspects, including "to identify and take action on influences which are critical to the health of marine ecosystems." The Arctic Council definition further includes this substantive aspect.[276] Other conceptualizations of the ecosystem approach that include substantive aspects are variants emphasizing "maintenance of ecosystem integrity"[277] or that "enable and ensure conservation of ecosystem service and take account of, or minimize, risks/threats to ecosystem function and structure."[278] These examples of substantive aspects concern actions or interventions ('maintain,' 'minimize,' 'identify and take action') combined with a desired outcome. Focusing on these or other substantive aspects of the

---

273 Convention on Biodiversity COP 5 Decision V/6, section B.

274 Elizabeth A. Kirk, "The Ecosystem Approach and the Search for An Objective and Content for the Concept of Holistic Ocean Governance," *Ocean Development & International Law* 46, no. 1 (2015).

275 OSPAR Commission, *Bergen Statement* (2010), source:https://www.ospar.org/site/assets/files/36552/bergen_statement.pdf, (last accessed 25 April 2023).

276 Arctic Council, *Kiruna Declaration* (2013), source: https://pame.is/projects/ecosystem-approach, (last accessed 25 April 2023).

277 Common statement by the Helsinki and OSPAR Commissions (2003), *Towards an Ecosystem Approach to the Management of Human Activities*, source: https://www.ospar.org/site/assets/files/1232/jmm_annex05_ecosystem_approach_statement.pdf (last accessed 25 April 2023).

278 Convention on Biodiversity COP 7 Decision VII/11.

ecosystem approach is one available avenue to unpack or further the substance of the ecosystem approach.

5.1.3 Responsiveness and Adaptability

The question for this section is what this theoretical framework has to offer to the responsiveness of governance and the adaptability inherent in the fundamental design of a governance instrument. The reality of responsive decision-making is challenged by the fact that human interference with the marine environment happens at multiple scales. The many problems of the (marine) environment are not controllable by any single decision maker. The impact on an area or ecosystem component results from a set of pressures or stressors (climate change, local and global pollution, area use), some local and some global.[279] This means that what to respond to, how to respond, and who should respond will often be unclear.

Insofar as existing knowledge on the status of the marine ecosystems arguably supports a range of existing different political positions, the question remains which inputs or influences trigger governance responses. For a simplified example, under a conservative government, will new knowledge that the ocean temperature keeps increasing trigger responses indicating those strategies that a green party would have adopted in the first place based on previous measurements? And how would a green party government respond? The extent to which a policy or regulation sets out that it should respond in the face of, for example, increasing ocean temperatures or red listing of a species, or, if a policy or regulation already accounts for an increasing ocean temperature, how to respond, is somewhat clarified up front. If, however, the policy or regulation does not mention the change of circumstance in the marine environment that new scientific evidence reflects, whether unforeseen or not planned for, a call to respond cannot be translated to a specific policy option.

The change of circumstance in the marine environment (such as, increased ocean temperature) could be used as an argument to respond by changing the fundamental design of existing policies and regulations, which likely invoke a particular decision-making procedure, such as a law-making process. The

279 The global scale is for example evident in that the "production of energy, the exploitation of resources, the transformation into goods and services, and the consumption thereof occur at a global scale, as resources, production facilities and end consumers often reside on each continent (...) Throughout this process, waste products are created. Further, the capacity of the biosphere to absorb or detoxify the substances resulting from these global processes is also global in scale," Schøning, "The Contribution of Integrated Marine Policies to Marine Environmental Protection: The Case of Norway", 6; Burger et al., "The Macroecology of Sustainability," 4.

change of circumstance could also be used as an argument to respond by changing individual decisions in terms of such policy or regulation, such as strengthening requirements of licenses to operate, relieving restrictions applicable to a marine protected area, or phasing out certain harmful activities. Such responses could be within the mandate and margin of appreciation of the relevant authority yet could also interfere with the rights and obligations of actors, which could pose a barrier or require certain procedures to be made. Further, to exemplify from the governance options end, which input or influence (including scientific evidence) would invoke revision of the set of international treaties that could facilitate circular economy or the regulatory devised objectives and priorities of economic actors? Such changes, argued as appropriate governance responses for better protecting the environment,[280] may require a change of political priorities rather than responsive governance.

Since the substance or merit of ocean governance perspective of this study has focused on the fundamental design of a governance instrument, another question is the flexibility provided for some subsequent adjustments (adaptivity) in the design. What space there is for adaptivity reflects which changes can and cannot be made without changing the partition and its fundamental design, as reflected in governance instruments and governance structures. As per Platjouw and Soininen, referring to governance instruments, "[a]daptivity may be built into the legal design of aquaculture or fisheries regulation, adaptivity may be fostered through iterative planning and licensing systems, and also the law-making process itself may be adaptive."[281] Adaptivity within the limits of the existing partition and governance instrument design may be possible, for example, against predefined criteria or within predefined limits.

However, as far as partition and design of governance instruments reflect institutional or organizational realities, suggested changes must take account of the institutional or organizational partitioning. For example, if we had increased eutrophication in a marine area, which policy options could it give rise to? For example, the restriction of nearby conventional agriculture or nearby conventional aquaculture, or the improvement of nearby waste-

280 Arguments for circularity, see for example, Sarah J. Morath, Our plastic problem and how to solve it (Cambridge: Cambridge University Press, 2022); Marilena Streit-Bianchi, Margarita Cimadevila, and Wolfgang Trettnak, *Mare Plasticum—The Plastic Sea: Combatting Plastic Pollution Through Science and Art*, 1st 2020. ed. (Cham: Springer International Publishing: Imprint: Springer, 2020); arguments for corporate reform, see for example, Beate Sjåfjell, "Redefining the Corporation for a Sustainable New Economy," *Journal of law and society* 45, no. 1 (2018): 29–45.

281 Platjouw and Soininen, "Reconciling the rule of law with adaptive regulation of marine ecosystems—Challenges and opportunities for the Arctic and beyond," 3.

water treatment facilities? How and to what extent? Building into the legal design adaptive capacity to handle such situations is at best challenging, as agriculture, aquaculture, and wastewater in most cases would be regulated by different instruments and different governance units. Moreover, the indirect drivers of problems challenge adaptation. For example, perhaps ocean warming is enhancing the effects of eutrophication,[282] to which uncertainty is attached and which raises the question of which activities or behavior lead to ocean warming as, perhaps, they need to be adapted.

This example shows how adaptivity in the design of one instrument is challenged, first, by the partitioning of governance instruments and institutions. Certainly, the partition and design of institutions and organizations may also be changed, as is sometimes appropriate and would require certain decision-making processes such as law-making processes. Second, the adaptivity in the design of one instrument is challenged by the problem at hand and the problem framing. Problems of a technical nature, which have an identifiable and given cause, such as visible or measurable impact of chemicals on the marine environment, used to treat farmed fish for parasites and emitted into the sea, may be adapted to, such as, by increasing or decreasing the limits for such emissions. Complicated or even complex problems are harder to adapt to. For example, if a shoal of shrimp nearby aquaculture farms is in poor condition, it may have multiple causes, some related to chemical emissions related to the nearby aquaculture farm and others not (such as, ocean warming). Even in this simple yet complex problem frame, what to adapt to, when, and how is comparably less straightforward and may demand experimentation.[283]

5.2 *Conclusions*

5.2.1 Governance and Its Interfaces with Science and Law

The systematic study by Jagannathan et al. of the assumptions on the science–policy interface and critical gaps in understanding of the science-society interface concluded that governance could be used as a lens for future studies.[284] In response, this study has used and has shown the appropriateness of using governance as a lens to investigate what is therefore the governance–science relationship, and, additionally, the governance–law

---

282 Pazzaglia et al., "Multiple stressors in P. oceanica."

283 Ronald A. Heifetz, Alexander Grashow, and Marty Linsky, *The practice of adaptive leadership: Tools and tactics for changing your organization and the world* (Boston, Mass: Harvard Business Press, 2009).

284 Jagannathan et al., "A research agenda for the science of actionable knowledge: Drawing from a review of the most misguided to the most enlightened claims in the science-policy interface literature."

relationships. The many ways of approaching governance entails that the "governance lens" is not a single lens, but multiple, and the way in which governance is approached has profound implications for the resulting interfaces to be investigated.

This study has approached governance in a manner that is specifically tailored to the ocean governance context. Nonetheless, the study has also led to results that are generic to governance in general. By using the given context and aiming to circle in the content of ocean governance, the study has provided a set of components—structures and processes; ideals and standards; substance or merit—that may be appropriate to the studying of any governance context. Arguably, much research on ocean governance focuses on (phases of) governance processes, governance structures, and ideals and standards. One intention of the undertaken governance perspective has been to investigate the substance of ocean governance, as provided for through a process of elimination of structures and processes, and ideals and standards, generic to governance.

The investigations have shown that the first component of governance structures and processes, and the related structural risks and governance process phases, are no different whether the matter is terrestrial or marine or whether the matter concerns facilitating defense interests or managing taxation or education. Further, the processes and structural risks are in theory no different if the governance unit is an organization, a state, a public entity, or a private company. Promoting generic characteristics and risks of any systems as solutions to, or ways forward for, ocean governance remains an incomplete exercise. While these inherent structural risks and processes of generic governance are also relevant to ocean governance, calls, for example, for coordination or participatory processes should justify or clarify what it is that we need to coordinate and why, why coordination is appropriate at the expense of other ways of enhancing integration in the ocean governance case at hand, and to what extent coordination will respond to the problem.

The investigations have further shown how the second component of ideals and standards of governance identifies certain ideals and standards that are typical for ocean governance. These ideals and standards include participation, integration, science-based decision-making, and the ecosystem approach. The investigations reveal how some of these ideals and standards involve ways of describing governance structures and processes. While these ideals and standards may be presented as universal or a necessity, this study argues that the relevance of such ideals and standards to any governance issue or research question arguably demands justification and specification of the limits of the ideal or standard.

The study has shown how the third component of governance, its substance or merit, could be approached in a number of ways, while this study has chosen to investigate the design of governance instruments. Unpacking the substantive component has been an exploratory undertaking. By investigating the how, what, who, and why of ocean governance, the approach has revealed different premises that may dictate the content of ocean governance. It remains to see whether the approach has carved out a research space—the substance of (ocean) governance.

The three-component governance perspective has further facilitated the mapping of what in these respects is a nuanced relationship between governance and science and governance and law. The governance–science relationship captures how science informs governance in multiple ways. They include how science contribute to enlightenment (such as in the general understanding of the Earth and the human needs); values (such as the extent to which we value and prioritize protecting the Arctic ice zone and other habitats and ecosystems depends on, inter alia, knowing about them); problem orientation (such as how we may identify knowledge gaps such as the limited knowledge of the seafloor); and to design and evaluation of policy and regulation (such as, by identifying resources to be exploited, such as seabed minerals, or ecosystem components to be protected, such as cold water reefs).

Despite these multiple ways in which science contributes to governance, science provides only some of many concerns informing governance. Other inputs and concerns beyond (marine) scientific input may concurrently compete for attention in ocean matters. These nonscientific and scientific inputs include concerns for employment, social distribution, economic prosperity, and perceptions of possibilities, including that of reelection. Moreover, and importantly, scientific input may give rise to multiple policy and regulatory alternatives, depending on, for example, political positions. In summary, the relevance of science to governance is in some ways broad, and in other ways limited.

The investigation of the relevance of law to governance has unpacked how legal structures resembles governance structures, and how governance instrument may equal legal instruments. Further, the investigation has shown how law serves different governance roles in modern states.[285] The first role is that of ordering power through establishing and distributing legal authority and power, which defines the formal governance structures. Further, the second role of law is its constitutive or foundational role of defining or framing multiple formal governance processes. These involve policy-making and law-making

---

285 Inspired by López-Calva and Zhou, *Governance and the law*, as section 4 explains in more detail.

processes and contestation processes. The third role of law for governance is that of ordering the behavior of individuals, organizations, or states. Typically, this is registered in governance instruments (policies and regulations) which provides an important premise for the substance or merit of governance. Accordingly, the roles of law for governance are many and vital.

5.2.2 The Emerging Field of Study of Ocean Governance

This study has aimed to instigate further discussion on, and development of, the theory of ocean governance. In building theoretical understanding of an understudied area, this study has contributed to the understanding of how governance could be approached in an ocean governance context; how science is relevant to ocean governance in various yet limited ways; and law's many roles relevant to ocean governance.

This study has arguably demonstrated that ocean governance is emerging as a field of study in its own right, embracing governance, science, and law as key and intertwined themes. Further, this study wishes to highlight that, beyond the marine focus and the focus on the generic governance components of structure and process, ocean governance is characterized by a set of common ideals and standards, and shared objectives. The ideals and standards set out that ocean governance should be participatory, integrated, ecosystem based (or based on an ecosystem approach), science based, and based on the rule of law. Shared objectives are the protection or preservation of marine ecosystems and the sustainable use of a marine resource or a marine area. Both the ideals and standards and the objectives reflect certain values. Therefore, ocean governance is characterized by certain focal areas and certain values, providing common framing, in which limits and possibilities are inherent.

The roles of law for ocean governance—ordering authority, framing processes, and ordering behavior—should not be underestimated. Law provides the formal infrastructure for governance and defines the governance processes where policy and law is created.[286] Further, permission to interfere with ecosystems, such as emission permits, resource use and outtake, new constructions, and area use, often require a hard legal basis, as does distribution of, and obtaining, individual rights to ecosystem components. The human interference with ocean ecosystem is therefore written in law, which preserves law's role as essential to ocean governance.

The amount of literature produced and the current spotlight on ocean governance practices, such as developing new governance instruments focusing on ocean governance, internationally and nationally, indicates that this emerging

---

286 See note 226 and section 4.

field of study may not be a passing trend but one that is here to stay. Scholars and policymakers framing research and policy initiatives as 'ocean governance' should nonetheless pay attention to the justification and limitations inherent in such frame. Hopefully, some of the future research on ocean governance will focus on exploring and developing the substance or merit of ocean governance, leading to progress in outcome in meeting the objectives of sustainably using and caring for the ocean.

Acknowledgement

Thanks are extended to my many friendly and clever colleagues at NCLOS—the Norwegian Centre for the Law of the Sea and across the faculties at UiT The Arctic University of Norway. This study is financed by the Research Council of Norway, through the project Developing Good Ocean Governance for the Arctic (DOGA).

Bibliography

Agardy, Tundi S. *Ocean Zoning: Making Marine Management More Effective*. London: Taylor & Francis Group, 2010.

Agreement under the United Nations Convention on the Law of the Sea on the Conservation and Sustainable Use of Marine Biological Diversity of Areas Beyond National Jurisdiction, Adopted 19 June 2023.

Alpizar, F., F. Carlsson, G. Lanza, B. Carney, R. C. Daniels, M. Jaime, T. Ho, *et al.* "A Framework for Selecting and Designing Policies to Reduce Marine Plastic Pollution in Developing Countries." *Environmental Science & Policy* 109 (2020): 25–35.

Arctic Council. *Kiruna Declaration* (2013),source: https://pame.is/projects/ecosystem-approach (last accessed 25 April 2023).

Armstrong, Kenneth Kilpatrick, Claire. "Law, Governance, or New Governance—the Changing Open Method of Coordination Narrowing the Gap: Law and New Approaches to Governance in the European Union." *Colum. J. Eur. L.* 13 (2006): 652–55.

Bacchi, Carol, and Susan Goodwin. "Making and Unmaking 'Problems'." In *Poststructural Policy Analysis: A Guide to Practice*, edited by Carol Bacchi and Susan Goodwin, 57–68. New York: Palgrave Macmillan US, 2016.

Bacchi, Carol Lee. *Analysing Policy: What's the Problem Represented to Be?* Frenchs Forest, NSW: Pearson Australia, 2009.

Baldwin, Amy, Bryce D. Bunting, Doug Daugherty, Latoya Lewis, and Timothy A. Steenbergh. *Promoting Belonging, Growth Mindset, and Resilience to Foster Student*

Success. Columbia, SC: National Resource Center for The First-Year Experience and Students in Transition, University of South Carolina, 2020.

Bardwell, Lisa V. "Problem-Framing: A Perspective on Environmental Problem-Solving." *Environmental Management* (*New York*) 15, no. 5 (1991): 603–12.

Bender, Morgan Lizabeth, Julia Giebichenstein, Ragnar N. Teisrud, Jennifer Laurent, Marianne Frantzen, James P. Meador, Lisbet Sørensen, *et al.* "Combined Effects of Crude Oil Exposure and Warming on Eggs and Larvae of an Arctic Forage Fish." *Sci Rep* 11, no. 1 (2021): 8410–17.

Bennett, Nathan James, Jessica Blythe, Carole Sandrine White, and Cecilia Campero. "Blue Growth and Blue Justice: Ten Risks and Solutions for the Ocean Economy." *Marine policy* 125 (2021): 104387.

Berghöfer, Augustin, Heidi Wittmer, and Felix Rauschmayer. "Stakeholder Participation in Ecosystem-Based Approaches to Fisheries Management: A Synthesis from European Research Projects." *Marine policy* 32, no. 2 (2008): 243–53.

Bernal, Patricio, Beatrice Ferreira, Lorna Inniss, Enrique Marschoff, Jake Rice, Andy Rosenberg, and Alan Simcock. "Chapter 54. Overall Assessment of Human Impacts on the Oceans." In *The First Global Integrated Marine Assessment—World Ocean Assessment I*, edited by Lorna Inniss, Alan Simcock, Amanuel Yoanes Ajawin, Angel C. Alcala, Patricio Bernal, Hilconida P. Calumpong, Peyman Eghtesadi Araghi and et al., 1–17: United Nations General Assembly, 2016.

Biermann, Frank, Casey Stevens, Steven Bernstein, Aarti Gupta, Norichika Kanie, Måns Nilsson, and Michelle Scobie. "Global Goal Setting for Improving National Governance and Policy." In *Governing through Goals*, 75, edited by Frank Biermann and Norichika Kanie. Sustainable Development Goals as Governance Innovation: The MIT Press, 2017.

Boesch, Donald F. "The Role of Science in Ocean Governance." *Ecological economics* 31, no. 2 (1999): 189–98.

Bohman, Brita. "Regulatory Control of Adaptive Fisheries: Reflections on the Implementation of the Landing Obligation in the Eu Common Fisheries Policy." *Marine Policy* 110 (2019): 103557.

Brodie Rudolph, Tanya, Mary Ruckelshaus, Mark Swilling, Edward H. Allison, Henrik Österblom, Stefan Gelcich, and Philile Mbatha. "A Transition to Sustainable Ocean Governance." *Nature Communications* 11, no. 1 (2020): 3600.

Brondízio, E. S., J. Settele, S. Díaz, and H. T. (eds) Ngo. *IPBES the Global Assessment Report on Biodiversity and Ecosystem Services, Summary for Policymakers* (Bonn, Germany: 2019), source: https://www.ipbes.net/global-assessment IPBES (last accessed 25 April 2023).

Brownlie, Ian. *Principles of Public International Law*. 7th ed. Oxford: Oxford University Press, 2008.

Brunnée, Jutta, and Stephen J. Toope. *Legitimacy and Legality in International Law: An Interactional Account*. Cambridge Studies in International and Comparative Law. Cambridge: Cambridge University Press, 2010.

Bueger, Christian, and Felix Mallin. "Blue Paradigms: Understanding the Intellectual Revolution in Global Ocean Politics." *International affairs* (London) 99, no. 4 (2023): 1719–39.

Burch, Sarah, Aarti Gupta, Cristina Y. A. Inoue, Agni Kalfagianni, Åsa Persson, Andrea K. Gerlak, Atsushi Ishii, *et al.* "New Directions in Earth System Governance Research." *Earth System Governance* 1 (2019): 100006.

Burger, Joseph R., Craig D. Allen, James H. Brown, William R. Burnside, Ana D. Davidson, Trevor S. Fristoe, Marcus J. Hamilton, et al. "The Macroecology of Sustainability." *PLoS Biology* 10, no. 6 (2012): e1001345.

Caldeira, Ken, and Michael E. Wickett. "Anthropogenic Carbon and Ocean Ph." *Nature* 425, no. 6956 (2003): 365–65.

Campbell, Lisa M., Luke Fairbanks, Grant Murray, Joshua S. Stoll, Linda D'Anna, and Julia Bingham. "From Blue Economy to Blue Communities: Reorienting Aquaculture Expansion for Community Wellbeing." *Marine policy* 124 (2021): 104361.

Celermajer, Danielle, David Schlosberg, Lauren Rickards, Makere Stewart-Harawira, Mathias Thaler, Petra Tschakert, Blanche Verlie, and Christine Winter. "Multispecies Justice: Theories, Challenges, and a Research Agenda for Environmental Politics." *Environmental politics* 30, no. 1–2 (2021): 119–40.

Chafetz, Josh. *Congress's Constitution: Legislative Authority and the Separation of Powers*. New Haven, CT: Yale University Press, 2017.

Charles, Anthony. "People, Oceans and Scale: Governance, Livelihoods and Climate Change Adaptation in Marine Social–Ecological Systems." *Current Opinion in Environmental Sustainability* 4, no. 3 (2012): 351–57.

Colombi Ciacchi, Aurelia, and Dietmar von der Pfordten. "Exploring the Relationship between Law and Governance: A Proposal." *The Theory and Practice of Legislation* 11, no. 2 (2023): 151–67.

Commissions, Common statement by the Helsinki and OSPAR (2003). *Towards an Ecosystem Approach to the Management of Human Activities*, source: https://www.ospar.org/site/assets/files/1232/jmm_annex05_ecosystem_approach_statement.pdf, last accessed 25 April 2023.

Convention for the Protection of the Marine Environment of the North-East Atlantic (OSPAR), adopted 22 September 1992, entered into force 25 March 1998, 2354 UNTS 67.

Convention on Biodiversity Conference of Parties 5 Decision V/6, available at https://www.cbd.int/decisions/ (last accessed 25 April 2023).

Convention on Biodiversity Conference of Parties 7 Decision VII/11, available at https://www.cbd.int/decisions/ (last accessed 25 April 2023).

Convention on Biological Diversity (CBD), adopted June 5, 1992, entered into force 29 December 1993, 1760 UNTS 79.

Convention on Environmental Impact Assessment in a Transboundary Context (Espoo Convention), adopted 25 February 1991, entered into force 10 September 1997, 1989 UNTS 309.

Cosens, Barbara, J. B. Ruhl, Niko Soininen, Lance Gunderson, Antti Belinskij, Thorsten Blenckner, Alejandro E. Camacho, *et al.* "Governing Complexity: Integrating Science, Governance, and Law to Manage Accelerating in the Commons." *Proceedings of the National Academy of Sciences—PNAS* 118, no. 36 (2021): 2102798118.

Davies, Margaret. "Theoretical Variables". In *Law Unlimited: Materialism, Pluralism and Legal Theory*, edited by Margaret Davies. London: Taylor and Francis, 2017: 1.

Declaration on the establishment of the Arctic Council (Ottawa Declaration) of 1996, source: http://hdl.handle.net/11374/85 (last accessed 25 April 2023).

Díaz, S., J. Settele, E. S. Brondízio, H. T. Ngo, M. Guèze, J. Agard, A. Arneth, and et al. *IPBES 2019: Summary for Policymakers of the Global Assessment Report on Biodiversity and Ecosystem Services (Summary for Policy Makers). IPBES Plenary at Its Seventh Session (IPBES 7, Paris, 2019).* IPBES (Bonn: Zenodo, 2019).

Dietz, Thomas, Elinor Ostrom, and Paul C. Stern. "The Struggle to Govern the Commons." *Science* 302, no. 5652 (2003): 1907–12.

Directive 2014/89/EU of the European Parliament and of the Council of 23 July 2014 Establishing a Framework for Maritime Spatial Planning, OJ L 257, 28.8.2014, 135–145. Source: http://data.europa.eu/eli/dir/2014/89/oj (last accessed 25 April 2023).

Dupont, Christophe, and Guy-Oliver Faure. "The Negotiation Process." *International negotiation* (1991): 40–57.

Ehler, Charles, Jacek Zaucha, and Kira Gee. "Maritime/Marine Spatial Planning at the Interface of Research and Practice," 614, In *Maritime Spatial Planning: Past, Present, Future*, edited by Jacek Zaucha and Kira Gee, 1–21. Cham: Palgrave Macmillan, 2019.

Etzioni, Amitai. "Introduction: Policy Research." *International Studies in Sociology and Social Anthropology*, vol. 26, (Leiden: Brill, 1978): 1–6.

Food and Agriculture Organization of the United Nations. "FAO Voluntary Guidelines for Securing Sustainable Small-Scale Fisheries in the Context of Food Security and Poverty Eradication." 2015.

Fukuyama, Francis. *Political Order and Political Decay: From the Industrial Revolution to the Globalization of Democracy*. London: Profile Books, 2014.

Fukuyama, Francis. "Transitions to the Rule of Law." *Journal of democracy* 21, no. 1 (2010): 33–44.

Gilek, Michael, Fred Saunders, and Ignė Stalmokaitė. "The Ecosystem Approach and Sustainable Development in Baltic Sea Marine Spatial Planning: The Social Pillar, a 'Slow Train Coming'," 160. In *The Ecosystem Approach in Ocean Planning and*

Governance, edited by David Langlet and Rosemary Rayfuse. Leiden, Boston: BRILL, 2018: 160.

Haas, Bianca, Mary Mackay, Camilla Novaglio, Liam Fullbrook, Michael Murunga, Carla Sbrocchi, Jan McDonald, *et al.* "The Future of Ocean Governance." *Reviews in Fish Biology and Fisheries* (2021): 1–18.

Hammer, Maria. "Lost in Translation—Following the Ecosystem Approach from Malawi to the Barents Sea," *Arctic Review on Law and Politics*, 14 (2023): 46–69.

Harari, Yuval N. *Sapiens: A Brief History of Humankind.* First U.S. edition. New York: Harper, 2015.

Hasselman, Lyndal. "Adaptive Management; Adaptive Co-Management; Adaptive Governance: What's the Difference?". *Australasian Journal of Environmental Management* 24, no. 1 (2017): 31–46.

Heifetz, Ronald A., Alexander Grashow, and Marty Linsky. *The Practice of Adaptive Leadership: Tools and Tactics for Changing Your Organization and the World.* Boston, Mass: Harvard Business Press, 2009.

Hennessey, Lawrence Juda Timothy. "Governance Profiles and the Management of the Uses of Large Marine Ecosystems." *Ocean Development & International Law* 32, no. 1 (2001): 43–69.

Hoppe, Robert. "Scientific Advice and Public Policy: Expert Advisers' and Policymakers' Discourses on Boundary Work." *Poiesis & Praxis* 6, no. 3 (2009): 235–63.

Inniss, Lorna, Alan Simcock, Amanuel Yoanes Ajawin, Angel C. Alcala, Patricio Bernal, Hilconida P. Calumpong, Peyman Eghtesadi Araghi, and et al. *The First Global Integrated Marine Assessment—World Ocean Assessment I*, United Nations (2016), source: https://www.un.org/regularprocess/content/first-world-ocean-assessment (last accessed 25 April 2023).

Integrated Management Plan for the Norwegian Marine Areas. Report Nr. 20 to the Storting 2019–2020, available at https://www.regjeringen.no/en/dokumenter/meld.-st.-20-20192020/id2699370/ (last accessed 4 November 2023).

Jagannathan, Kripa, Geniffer Emmanuel, James Arnott, Katharine J. Mach, Aparna Bamzai-Dodson, Kristen Goodrich, Ryan Meyer, *et al.* "A Research Agenda for the Science of Actionable Knowledge: Drawing from a Review of the Most Misguided to the Most Enlightened Claims in the Science-Policy Interface Literature." *Environmental science & policy* 144 (2023): 174–86.

Jans, Jan H. "Stop the Integration Principle." *Fordham International Law Journal* 33, no. 5 (2010): 1533–47.

Jasanoff, Sheila. *The Fifth Branch: Science Advisers as Policymakers.* Cambridge, Mass: Harvard University Press, 1990.

Jasanoff, Sheila. *States of Knowledge: The Co-Production of Science and the Social Order.* International Library of Sociology. Abingdon, Oxon: Routledge, 2004.

Johansen, Elise. "The EU Influence on Norwegian Domestic Legislation for the Protection of the Arctic Marine Environment." *The International Journal of Marine and Coastal Law* 33, no. 2 (2018): 415–35.

Jones, Peter J. S., L. M. Lieberknecht, and W. Qiu. "Marine Spatial Planning in Reality: Introduction to Case Studies and Discussion of Findings." *Marine Policy* 71 (2016): 256–64.

Juda, Lawrence, and Timothy Hennessey. "Governance Profiles and the Management of the Uses of Large Marine Ecosystems." Ocean Development & International Law 32, no. 1 (2001): 43–69.

Justesen, Lise, and Nanna Mik-Meyer. *Qualitative Research Methods in Organisation Studies*. Copenhagen: Hans Reitzels Forl., 2012.

Kaiser, Michel J., Martin Attrill, Simon Jennings, David N. Thomas, David K. A. Barnes, Andrew Brierley, Nicholas A. J. Graham, *et al. Marine Ecology: Processes, Systems, and Impacts*. Third edition. ed. Oxford, England: Oxford University Press, 2020.

Kanetake, Machiko, and André Nollkaemper. *The Rule of Law at the National and International Levels: Contestations and Deference*. Oxford, Portland, Oregon: Hart Publishing Ltd, 2016.

Kelly, Christina, Lorraine Gray, Rachel J. Shucksmith, and Jacqueline F. Tweddle. "Investigating Options on How to Address Cumulative Impacts in Marine Spatial Planning." *Ocean & Coastal Management* 102 (2014): 139–48.

Kirk, Elizabeth A. "The Ecosystem Approach and the Search for an Objective and Content for the Concept of Holistic Ocean Governance." *Ocean Development & International Law* 46, no. 1 (2015): 33–49.

Klein, Natalie, and Kate Parlett. *Judging the Law of the Sea*. Oxford, United Kingdom: Oxford University Press, Incorporated, 2023.

Klinger, Dane H., Anne Maria Eikeset, Brynhildur Davíðsdóttir, Anna-Marie Winter, and James R. Watson. "The Mechanics of Blue Growth: Management of Oceanic Natural Resource Use with Multiple, Interacting Sectors." *Marine Policy* 87 (2018): 356–62.

Komatsu, Teruhisa, Hubert-Jean Ceccaldi, Jiro Yoshida, Patrick Prouzet, and Yves Henocque. *Oceanography Challenges to Future Earth: Human and Natural Impacts on Our Seas*. 1st 2019. ed. Cham: Springer International Publishing: Imprint: Springer, 2019.

Kooiman, Jan. *Governing as Governance*. London: London: SAGE Publications, 2003.

Kooiman, Jan, and Maarten Bavinck. "The Governance Perspective." In *Fish for Life: Interactive Governance for Fisheries*, edited by Jan Kooiman, Maarten Bavinck, Roger Pullin and Svein Jentoft, Amsterdam University Press, 2005: 11.

Kornhauser, Lewis A. "Law as an Achievement of Governance." [In English]. *Journal of Legal Philosophy* 47, no. 1 (01 May 2022): 1–23.

Kyrönviita, Jonas, David Langlet, Niko Soininen, Antti Belinskij, Sara Kymenvaara, and Ellen Margrethe Basse. "Achieving Blue Growth Post-Weser: A Study of Aquaculture

Regulation in the Nordic Region." *Journal for European environmental & planning law* 2021, 18, no. 3 (2021): 256–74.

Lamy, Pascal, Antidia Citores, Alan Deidun, Lowri Evans, François Galgani, Peter Heffernan, Aristomenis Karageorgis, and et al. *Proposed Mission: Mission Starfish 2030: Restore Our Ocean and Waters*. Report of the Mission Board Healthy Oceans, Seas, Coastal and Inland Waters (2020).

Langlet, David. "Scale, Space and Delimitation in Marine Legal Governance—Perspectives from the Baltic Sea." *Marine Policy* 98 (2018): 278–85.

Langlet, David, and Rosemary Rayfuse. "The Ecosystem Approach in Ocean Planning and Governance: An Introduction." In *The Ecosystem Approach in Ocean Planning and Governance*, edited by David Langlet and Rosemary Rayfuse. Perspectives from Europe and Beyond, 1–14. Leiden: BRILL, 2019.

Long, Rachel D., Anthony Charles and Robert L. Stephenson, "Key Principles of Marine Ecosystem-Based Management," *Marine Policy* 57 (2015): 53–60.

López-Calva, Luis Felipe, and Yongmei Zhou. *Governance and the Law*. Washington, District of Columbia: World Bank Group 2017.

Lynch, Richard. *Corporate Strategy*. 2nd ed. Harlow: Financial Times, 2000.

MacDonald, Bertrum H., Suzuette S. Soomai, Elizabeth M. De Santo, and Peter G. Wells. *Science, Information, and Policy Interface for Effective Coastal and Ocean Management*. Milton, United Kingdom: Taylor & Francis Group, 2016.

MacDonald, Bertrum H. *Science, Information, and Policy Interface for Effective Coastal and Ocean Management*. Boca Raton, Fla.: CRC Press, 2016.

MacDonald, Bertrum H., Suzuette S. Soomai, Elizabeth M. De Santo, and Peter G. Wells. "Introduction." Chap. 1 In *Science, Information, and Policy Interface for Effective Coastal and Ocean Management*, edited by Bertrum H. MacDonald, Suzuette S. Soomai, Elizabeth M. De Santo and Peter G. Wells. Boca Raton, Florida: CRC Press, 2016: 3.

MacDonald, Bertrum H. "Understanding the Science–Policy Interface in Integrated Coastal and Ocean Management." Chap. 3 In *Science, Information, and Policy Interface for Effective Coastal and Ocean Management*, edited by Bertrum H. MacDonald, Suzuette S. Soomai, Elizabeth M. De Santo and Peter G. Wells. Boca Raton, Florida: CRC Press, 2016: 47.

Marine Resources Act of Norway. Lov om forvaltning av viltlevande marine ressursar (Havressurslova) Lov-2008-06-06-37. Oslo: Lovdata, 2008.

Martin, Josh. "A Transnational Law of the Sea." *Chicago journal of international law* 21, no. 2 (2021): 419–75.

Masson-Delmotte, V., P. Zhai, A. Pirani, S. L. Connors, C. Péan, S. Berger, N. Caud, *et al. Ipcc, 2021: Climate Change 2021: The Physical Science Basis. Contribution of Working Group I to the Sixth Assessment Report of the Intergovernmental Panel on Climate Change*. Cambridge University Press (Cambridge and New York: 2021).

McConney, Patrick, Lucia Fanning, Robin Mahon, and Bertha Simmons. "A First Look at the Science-Policy Interface for Ocean Governance in the Wider Caribbean Region." *Frontiers in Marine Science* 2 (2016): fmars.2015.00119.

Meadows, Donella H., and Diana Wright. *Thinking in Systems: A Primer*. White River Junction, Vermont: Earthscan, 2009.

Michalski, Joseph H. "The Sociological Determinants of Scientific Bias." *Journal of Moral Education* 51, no. 1 (2022): 47–60.

Monaco, André and Patrick Prouzet. *The Land-Sea Interactions*. Of *Oceanography and Marine Biology Series. Seas and Oceans Set.* (London: John Wiley & Sons, Incorporated, 2014).

Montevideo Convention on the Rights and Duties of States, adopted 26 December 1933, entered into force 26 December 1934, 1761 UNTS.

Morath, Sarah J. *Our Plastic Problem and How to Solve It.* Cambridge: Cambridge University Press, 2022.

OSPAR Commission. *Bergen Statement* (2010), source https://www.ospar.org/site/assets/files/36552/bergen_statement.pdf (last accessed 25 April 2023).

Páez, Daniela Pedroza, Luis A. Bojórquez-Tapia, Gian Carlo Delgado Ramos, and Elena Lazos Chavero. "Understanding Translation: Co-Production of Knowledge in Marine Spatial Planning." *Ocean & Coastal Management* 190 (2020): 105163.

Pahl-Wostl, Claudia. "A Conceptual Framework for Analysing Adaptive Capacity and Multi-Level Learning Processes in Resource Governance Regimes." *Global Environmental Change* 19, no. 3 (2009): 354–65.

Papanicolopulu, Irini. *Gender and the Law of the Sea.* 1 ed. Vol. 88, Boston: Boston: BRILL, 2019.

Pazzaglia, Jessica, Alex Santillán-Sarmiento, Stephanie B. Helber, Miriam Ruocco, Antonio Terlizzi, Lázaro Marín-Guirao, and Gabriele Procaccini. "Does Warming Enhance the Effects of Eutrophication in the Seagrass Posidonia Oceanica?" *Frontiers in Marine Science* 7 (2020): fmars-07-564805.

Pielke, Roger A. *The Honest Broker: Making Sense of Science in Policy and Politics.* Cambridge: Cambridge University Press, 2007.

Platjouw, Froukje Maria, and Niko Soininen. "Reconciling the Rule of Law with Adaptive Regulation of Marine Ecosystems—Challenges and Opportunities for the Arctic and Beyond." *Marine policy* 110 (2019): 103726.

Pörtner, H.-O., D. C. Roberts, V. Masson-Delmotte, P. Zhai, M. Tignor, E. Poloczanska, K. (eds.) Mintenbeck, et al. Ipcc 2019: Summary for Policymakers. In: *IPCC Special Report on the Ocean and Cryosphere in a Changing Climate* (*IPCC Special Report*), IPCC (Geneva, Switzerland: 2019), available at https://www.ipcc.ch/srocc/ (last accessed 25 April 2023).

Poto, Margherita Paola. *Enviromental Law and Governance: The Helicoidal Pathway of Participation; a Study of a Nature-Based Model Inspired by the Arctic, the Ocean, and Indigenous Views*. Torino: Giappichelli, 2022.

Quist, Johan, and Andreas Hellström. "Process Management as a Contagious Idea: A Contribution to Røvik's Virus-Inspired Theory." *International Journal of Public Administration* 35, no. 13 (2012): 901–13.

Rajamani, Lavanya. "The 2015 Paris Agreement: Interplay between Hard, Soft and Non-Obligations." *Journal of Environmental Law* 28, no. 2 (2016): 337–58.

Regime Interaction in International Law: Facing Fragmentation. Edited by Margaret A. Young. Cambridge: Cambridge University Press, 2012.

Rhodes, R. A. W. "Understanding Governance: Ten Years On." *Organization studies* 28, no. 8 (2007): 1243–64.

Rockström, J., W. Steffen, K. Noone, A. Persson, Fs Chapin, E. Lambin, T. M. Lenton, *et al.* "Planetary Boundaries: Exploring the Safe Operating Space for Humanity." *Ecol. Soc.* (2009): 32.

Rockström, J. "Planetary Boundaries." *New Perspectives Quarterly* 27, no. 1 (2010): 72–74.

Røvik, Kjell Arne. "Translasjon—En Alternativ Doktrine for Implementering." In *Reformideer i norsk skole: spredning, oversettelse og implementering*, edited by Kjell Arne Røvik, Tor Vidar Eilertsen and Eli Moksnes Furu. Oslo: Cappelen Damm akademisk, 2014: 403.

Rudd, Murray A. "Scientists' Framing of the Ocean Science–Policy Interface." *Global environmental change* 33 (2015): 44–60.

Rudd, Murray A., Mark Dickey-Collas, Johanna Ferretti, Ellen Johannesen, Nicol M. Macdonald, Richard McLaughlin, Margaret Rae, Torsten Thiele, and Jason S. Link. "Ocean Ecosystem-Based Management Mandates and Implementation in the North Atlantic." *Frontiers in Marine Science* 5 (2018): Article 458.

Ruhl, J. B., Barbara Cosens, and Niko Soininen. "Resilience of Legal Systems: Toward Adaptive Governance." In *Multisystemic Resilience*, edited by Michael Ungar. New York: Oxford Academic, 2021, 509.

Russell, Roseanne. "Companies and Unconscious Bias: A Case Study on the Need for Interdisciplinary Scholarship." In *Interdisciplinary Research for Sustainable Business: Perspectives of Women Business Scholars*, edited by Beate Sjåfjell, Roseanne Russell and Maja Van der Velden, 169. Cham: Springer International Publishing, 2023.

Ruwa, Renison, Alan Simcock, Jörn Schmidt, and et al. *The Second World Ocean Assessment—World Ocean Assessment II*. 2021, available at https://www.un.org/regularprocess/woa2launch (last accessed 25 April 2023).

Ryabinin, Vladimir, Julian Barbière, Peter Haugan, Gunnar Kullenberg, Neville Smith, Craig McLean, Ariel Troisi, and et al. "The Un Decade of Ocean Science for Sustainable Development." Policy and Practice Reviews. *Frontiers in Marine Science* 6, no. 470 (2019): fmars.2019.00470.

Salomon, Markus, and Till Markus. *Handbook on Marine Environment Protection: Science, Impacts and Sustainable Management.* Cham: Cham: Springer International Publishing, 2018.

Sander, Gunnar. "Against All Odds? Implementing a Policy for Ecosystem-Based Management of the Barents Sea." *Ocean & Coastal Management* 157 (2018/05/01/ 2018): 111–23.

Sander, Gunnar. "Implementation of Ecosystem-Based Ocean Management." (PhD diss., UiT The Arctic University of Norway, 2018).

Sands, Philippe, Jacqueline Peel, Adriana Fabra, and Ruth Mackenzie. *Principles of International Environmental Law.* 4th ed. Cambridge: Cambridge University Press, 2018.

Santos, Catarina, Tundi Agardy, Francisco Andrade, Helena Calado, Larry Crowder, Charles Ehler, Sara García-Morales, *et al.* "Integrating Climate Change in Ocean Planning." *Nature Sustainability* 3 (2020): 505–16.

Saunders, Fred P., Michael Gilek, and Ralph Tafon. "Adding People to the Sea: Conceptualizing Social Sustainability in Maritime Spatial Planning." In *Maritime Spatial Planning: Past, Present, Future*, edited by Jacek Zaucha and Kira Gee, 175–99. Cham: Palgrave Macmillan, 2019.

Schøning, Lena. "The Contribution of Integrated Marine Policies to Marine Environmental Protection: The Case of Norway." *International Journal of Marine and Coastal Law* 2 (2021): 263–93.

Schøning, Lena. "A Critical Assessment of the Contribution of Integrated Ocean Management to Protection of the Marine Environment." PhD, UiT The Arctic University of Norway, 2021.

Schøning, Lena, "A Methodology to Evaluate the Ecosystem Approach in Laws and Policies," Iva Parlov and Endalew Lijalem Enyew eds. *NCLOS blog. Norwegian Centre for the Law of the Sea*, 2022.

Schøning, Lena. "More or Less Integrated Ocean Management: Multiple Integrated Approaches and Two Norms." *Ocean Development & International Law* 51, no. 2 (2019): 95–115.

Schøning, Lena, Vera Helene Hausner, and Mathilde Morel. "Law and Sustainable Transitions: An Analysis of Aquaculture Regulation." *Environmental Innovation and Societal Transitions* 48 (2023/09/01/ 2023): 100753.

Science Advice for Policy by European Academies, SAPEA. *Making Sense of Science under Conditions of Complexity and Uncertainty.* (Berlin: SAPEA, 2019).

Scott, Karen N. "Integrated Oceans Management: A New Frontier in Marine Environmental Protection." Chap. 21 In *Oxford Handbook of the Law of the Sea*, edited by Donald R. Rothwell, Alex G. Oude Elferink, Karen N. Scott and Tim Stephens, 463. Oxford: Oxford University Press, 2015.

Severinsen, Greg. "Oceans Reform in Aotearoa New Zealand: A Just Transition?". *Policy Quarterly* 17, no. 3 (2021): 45–53.

Shelton, Dinah. "Soft Law." In *Routledge Handbook of International Law*, edited by David Armstrong, 68–80. London: Taylor & Francis, 2009.

Singh, Pradeep, and Aline Jaeckel. "Future Prospects of Marine Environmental Governance." In *Handbook on Marine Environment Protection: Science, Impacts and Sustainable Management*, edited by Markus Salomon and Markus Till. Cham: Palgrave Macmillan, 2018: 621.

Sjåfjell, Beate. "Redefining the Corporation for a Sustainable New Economy." *Journal of law and society* 45, no. 1 (2018): 29–45.

Sjåfjell, Beate. "Redefining Agency Theory to Internalize Environmental Product Externalities." In *Preventing Environmental Damage from Products: An Analysis of the Policy and Regulatory Framework in Europe*, edited by Carl Dalhammar, Eléonore Maitre-Ekern and Hans Christian Bugge, 101–24. Cambridge: Cambridge University Press, 2018.

Sjåfjell, Beate. "Towards a Sustainable Development: Internalising Externalities in Norwegian Company Law." *International and Comparative Corporate Law Journal* 6, no. 1 (November 21, 2010): 103–136.

Steel, Daniel. *Philosophy and the Precautionary Principle: Science, Evidence, and Environmental Policy*. Cambridge: Cambridge University Press, 2014.

Stelzenmüller, Vanessa, Patricia Breen, Tammy Stamford, Frank Thomsen, Fabio Badalamenti, Ángel Borja, Lene Buhl-Mortensen, *et al.* "Monitoring and Evaluation of Spatially Managed Areas: A Generic Framework for Implementation of Ecosystem Based Marine Management and Its Application." *Marine Policy* 37 (2013): 149–64.

Stephenson, Robert L., Alistair J. Hobday, Edward H. Allison, Derek Armitage, Kate Brooks, Alida Bundy, Christopher Cvitanovic, *et al.* "The Quilt of Sustainable Ocean Governance: Patterns for Practitioners." *Frontiers in Marine Science* 8 (2021): 630547.

Streit-Bianchi, Marilena, Margarita Cimadevila, and Wolfgang Trettnak. *Mare Plasticum—the Plastic Sea: Combatting Plastic Pollution through Science and Art*. 1st 2020. ed. Cham: Springer International Publishing: Imprint: Springer, 2020.

Takei, Yoshinobu. *A Sketch of the Concept of Ocean Governance and Its Relationship with the Law of the Sea*. Nova Et Vetera Iuris Gentium. Edited by Cedric Ryngaert, Erik J. Molenaar and Sarah M. H. Nouwen. Vol. 27, 2015: 48.

Teitel, Ruti. "Transitional Jurisprudence: The Role of Law in Political Transformation." *Yale L.J.* 106 (1996): 2009–2080.

Tijssen, Robert J. W. "Discarding the 'Basic Science/Applied Science' Dichotomy: A Knowledge Utilization Triangle Classification System of Research Journals." *Journal of the American Society for Information Science and Technology* 61, no. 9 (2010): 1842–52.

Trevisanut, Seline, and et al. *Regime Interaction in Ocean Governance*. Edited by Seline Trevisanut and et al. Boston: Boston: Brill, 2020.

Twining, William. "Jurisprudence: A Personal View." In *Jurist in Context: A Memoir* Cambridge: Cambridge University Press, 2019.

UN Secretary-General. "Secretary-General Calls Latest Ipcc Climate Report 'Code Red for Humanity', Stressing 'Irrefutable' Evidence of Human Influence." news release, 2021.

UN Secretary-General S/2004/616. *The Rule of Law and Transitional Justice in Conflict and Post-Conflict Societies*. United Nations (New York: 2004).

UN/CBD/COP/15/L25. "Kunming-Montreal Global Biodiversity Framework." 2022.

UNCLOS. United Nations Convention on the Law of the Sea, adopted 10 December 1982, entered into force 16 November 1994, 1833 UNTS 397.

UNESCO-IOC. *The Science We Need for the Ocean We Want*. Intergovernmental Oceanographic Commission (Paris, France: 2020).

United Nations Decade of Ocean Science for Sustainable Development (2021–2030). https://en.unesco.org/ocean-decade (last accessed 25 April 2023).

UNGA/Conf.48/14/Rev.1 Report of the United Nations Conference on the Human Environment (Stockholm Declaration). 1972.

UNGA/Conf.151/26 (Vol. I) Rio Declaration on Environment and Development. 1992.

United Nations Convention on the Law of the Sea of 10 December 1982, 1833 *U.N.T.S.* 3.

Varjopuro, Riku. "Evaluation of Marine Spatial Planning: Valuing the Process, Knowing the Impacts." In *Maritime Spatial Planning: Past, Present, Future*, edited by Jacek Zaucha and Kira Gee, 417. Cham: Palgrave Macmillan, 2019.

Varuhas, Jason N. E. "The Principle of Legality." *C.L.J.* 79, no. 3 (2020): 578–614.

Vienna Convention on the Law of Treaties. Treaty Series 1155 (May): 331.

Weiss, Carol H. "Knowledge Creep and Decision Accretion." *Knowledge* 1, no. 3 (1980): 381–404.

Weiss, Carol H. "The Many Meanings of Research Utilization." *Public administration review* 39, no. 5 (1979): 426–31.

Westerman, Pauline. "Governing by Goals: Governance as a Legal Style." *Legisprudence* 1, no. 1 (2007): 51–72.

Will, Steffen, Katherine Richardson, Johan Rockström, Sarah Cornell, Ingo Fetzer, Elena Bennett, Reinette Biggs, *et al.* "Planetary Boundaries: Guiding Human Development on a Changing Planet." *Science* 347, no. 6223 (2015): 736–736.

Winby, Stuart, and Christopher G. Worley. "Management Processes for Agility, Speed, and Innovation." *Organizational Dynamics* 43, no. 3 (2014): 225–34.

Winther, Jan-Gunnar, Minhan Dai, Therese Rist, Alf Håkon Hoel, Yangfan Li, Amy Trice, Karyn Morrissey, *et al.* "Integrated Ocean Management for a Sustainable Ocean Economy." *Nature Ecology & Evolution* 4 (2020): 1451–58.

Wolters, Erika Allen, Brent S. Steel, Denise Lach, and Daniel Kloepfer. "What Is the Best Available Science? A Comparison of Marine Scientists, Managers, and Interest Groups in the United States." *Ocean & coastal management* 122 (2016): 95–102.

Woolaston, Katie. *Ecological Vulnerability: The Law and Governance of Human–Wildlife Relationships*. Cambridge: Cambridge University Press, 2022.

Yin, Robert K. *Case Study Research and Applications: Design and Methods*. 6th ed. Los Angeles: SAGE, 2018.

Young, Margaret A. "Regime Interaction in Creating, Implementing and Enforcing International Law." In *Regime Interaction in International Law: Facing Fragmentation*, edited by Margaret A. Young, 85–110. Cambridge: Cambridge University Press, 2012.

Young, Oran R. *On Environmental Governance: Sustainability, Efficiency, and Equity*. New York: Routledge, 2016.

Zartman, William. "Negotiation as a Joint Decision-Making Process." *Journal of Conflict Resolution* 21, no. 4 (1977): 619–38.

www.ingramcontent.com/pod-product-compliance
Lightning Source LLC
Chambersburg PA
CBHW031330230926
51848CB00001B/169
9789004720251